C000272529

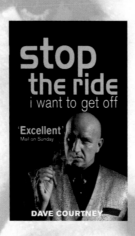

DODGY DAVE'S
LITTLE BLACK BOOK

DODGY DAVE'S
LITTLE BLACK BOOK

DAVE COURTNEY

Dedicated to my mum, my brother
Patrick and my sister Sue.

First published in 2001 by
Virgin Books
Thames Wharf Studios
Rainville Road
London
W6 9HA

A catalogue record for the book is available from
the British Library.

ISBN 0 7535 0685 8

Printed and bound by Omnia Books Ltd

CONTENTS

*He will cause his wife, his mother
and the police a lot of heartache!*
Mr Gerrard (my old headmaster)

INTRODUCTION

You know, I'm a firm believer in the fact that people are born naughty. I've never used no excuses for my naughtiness, like I weren't breastfed from the right tit. Or even the left one. I don't know whether I did cause a lot of grief for my wives, my mum and the police, you'd have to ask them — they're the ones all stood behind me nodding, by the way. But I think I made up for any of that by showing them a fucking funny time as well, along the way (the Old Bill might disagree with that but fuck 'em).

Whatever I'd done with my life I would've still been me. Still naughty. I could've become a priest, but I'd have been the naughtiest priest in church, drinking the wine, eating the bread and shagging a nun in the confessional. In fact, the more I think about it . . . no, maybe not, actually. It'd have been too difficult to justify the knuckleduster!

Crime has gone through changes over the years. It goes through different fashions just like clothes do. Certain values remain the same though, you can rely on that. Or used to be able to, anyway. But even that's got fucked up these days. 'Honour among thieves' works among thieves, but there's precious little honour among drug dealers.

I got out of my involvement while the getting was still good. As fate would have it I came out just as the world decided it was interested in 'gangster chic', or whatever you wanna call it, and my face fits in that. Or, 'cos I'm a saucy cunt – 'Gangster Cheek'.

Funnily enough the biggest new breed of robbers are ones who also wear pinstripe suits like the old-time gangsters did: and these new fellas in town are the City Boys and money traders who can nick more in ten minutes than ten thousand Great Train Robberies. Besides, how could you have a train robbery these days? You'd be waiting hours for the bastard thing to arrive.

Anyway, here we go. Another ride in the CourtneyWorld.

Small but perfectly formed, this book. Like a spider. Or a landmine. Or a spider landing on a landmine and getting itself blown the fuck to bits. Which would be fine by me 'cos I hate the little eight-legged crawly bastards. That's my biggest fear, spiders. I'd rather face ten men with an iron bar than a spider. What gets me about them is the way that when a spider spots you, first it stops . . . and then it runs *towards* you! What the fuck's that about?! You're a thousand times *bigger* than the little bastard! If you were out and about and you bumped into a spider that was a thousand times bigger than you, you wouldn't fucking run towards it, would you? It makes me think that they know something we don't, like a lot more of them are poisonous than we actually know. Sneaky little bastards. (While we're on the subject. Spiderman! Do me a favour. Spiderman as a hero? Crawling cunt.)

Anyway, like they say, there is nothing to fear but fear itself . . . and my missus with the hump.

Fuck me, I came over all poetic there for a second. Maybe I better cut down on the old E numbers. Yeah, I think I'll only do five next time I go raving.

Anyway, you know all those self-help books, the ones written mostly by Yanks, with titles like *How to Love Yourself*, *Get in Touch with Your Inner Child* and all that kind of crap? Well, guess what? This ain't one of them. This is *not* a self-help book, in fact it's more of a 'help yourself' book. So if you feel like nicking it, go ahead. Which reminds me, *Stop the Ride I Want to Get Off* is, officially, the most nicked book in the country. Is that a compliment or what? People are actually risking getting nabbed just because they want to read the book so much. I think you could say that I've successfully attracted a completely different clientele to the bookshop world.

I am going to do some of those self-help-type books myself, though. See what you think: *Getting in Touch with Your Inner Lesbian*, *How to Love Thy Neighbour and Not Get Caught*, *The Little Book of Harm*,

101 things to Do on Remand, *Raising Bail in 10 Easy Lessons*, *Wankers Paradise*; and my version of all the DIY/home decorating books, but this one's for prisoners, it's called *Changing Cells*. Good, eh? Also, a book for all those people who are fucked-off to the back teeth with those TV cooks, *How to Cook Jamie Oliver*. Tell me that ain't gonna be a big seller!

And, last but not least, my absolute favourite, *How to Spot a Bent Copper*. So a little something for everyone there, I think you'll agree.

Got the Mormons knocking on my door the other day, bang! bang! bang! for hours, they wouldn't give up. Eventually I had to let them out! Big-haired, Osmond-fondling bastards. They'd knocked on the door that morning and asked me if I'd ever thought of God. I said, Yeah, every time someone had shot at me. So I invited them all in and 'cos I'd just come in from going out clubbing six weeks ago — and I was still proper buzzing — I sat them down for a talk. Or, more accurately, a fucking good listen.

To be honest, I *was* ready to let God in my life, but there's absolutely no room. I've already got six sleeping on the front-room floor. But I am on a health kick now. I'm smoking herbal cigars. They're made from the remains of sundried vegetarians. Anyway, my body *is* a temple. That's why my shoes always stay on the outside.

I've had a rollercoaster of a year since I last saw you. Loads happened. I got nicked, got tried, got found innocent, got lied about by the police and some newspapers. Usual stuff. They really did try to stick it to me good and proper over the last year. But I came out on top, as I always try to. One thing I did learn was how being popular with one group can make you fucking unpopular with another. Meaning, that the more you people buy my books, read my column, watch my films, read my website, come to my 'Audience withs', etc., then the more the Metropolitan police get fucked off that their 'Crime Doesn't Pay' message starts to look a little ropey.

Funny thing is, when you read certain parts of *this* book you'll find that I'm actually putting across a message about crime that you might find surprising. Read on . . .

Dave Courtney OBE

1 THE VERBAL

- **ACTUAL BODILY HARM** – ABH

- **AGGRAVATION** – ag, proper ag, bother

- **ARMED** – tooled up, carrying, holding, cocked, lumped up

- **ARRESTED** – nicked, nabbed, lifted, took in, done, collar felt, pulled, pinched

- **BARRISTER** – brief

- **BLOKE** – boysie, geezer or geez, my son, bruv or bro, cocker, champ

- **BLOOD** – claret

- **BULLETS** – grub, food, little things, shells, bits

- **BULLET HOLE** – belly button, plug

- **CANNABIS/MARIJUANA** – grass, home-grown, puff, skunk, weed, joint, leb, bush, moroccan, black

- **CHAT (AGGRESSIVE)** – volleying off, raving, frothing, hollerin' and hootin', vexing

- **CHAT (FRIENDLY)** – verbal, chinwag, natter

- **COCAINE** – charlie, coke, powder, dandruff, marching powder, snow
- **DRUGS** – gear
- **ECSTASY** – little fellas, pills
- **FAKE** – moody
- **FAKE EVIDENCE** – stitch up, verballed, bugged, shafted
- **FIGHTING SKILL** – tasty, a tool, naughty bit of work, lethal
- **A FIGHT** – row, punch-up, straightener, scrap, tear-up
- **GANG** – firm
- **GANGED TOGETHER** – firm-handed
- **GANG'S AREA** – manor
- **GBH** – grevious bodily harm
- **GUN** – shooter, iron, tool, yoga, thing, rod
- **GYPSY** – pikey, tinker, doodi, traveller, Romany
- **HEROIN** – brown, skag, H
- **ILLEGAL ACTIVITY** – bit of work, on a job

- ◈ **HOUSE OR HOME** – gaff (as in the magazine *Gaff & Gardens*)
- ◈ **INFLUENCE** – clout, big say, power
- ◈ **JAIL** – nick, big house, slammer, chokey
- ◈ **JAIL SENTENCE** – bird, term, stretch, lagging, stir, time, porridge, banged-up
- ◈ **LUCK** – touch!, sweet, tops, wicked
- ◈ **MURDER** – top, cap, done, whacked, iron (as in 'iron girder')
- ◈ **SEXY YOUNG LADY** – a sort, doll, babe, ream, little darlin'
- ◈ **POLICE** – the Old Bill, gavvers, cozzers, rozzers, plod, pigs, filth, feds, the other lot, on top, babylon
- ◈ **CORRUPT POLICE** – bent Old Bill, mole, plant, for rent
- ◈ **PRISON OFFICER** – screw (bless!), cunt, oi you!
- ◈ **PROSTITUTE** – brass, tart, top tart, whore, tom, hooker
- ◈ **PUNCH** – clump, dig, smack
- ◈ **RENOWNED CHARACTER** – face
- ◈ **RESPECTED VILLAIN** – chap, guv, big noise, proper, good stuff

2 LIFE OF CRIME VS THE FAME GAME

'Celebrity gangster' is a funny old fucking phrase really. It's what they call a contradiction in terms. Like 'police intelligence' or 'football villain'. It don't make sense 'cos you can only be one or the other, not both. But if that's the name they want to use then that's OK. It sells.

I'm a pretty good long-term thinker. I remember what might have happened ten years ago to lead to this. I know what something can lead to even ten years down the line. A lot of people just live for today. Much as it may seem that I'm very carefree and with a 'don't give a monkey's' attitude to everything — well, actually I do.

I loved the romance of crime right from the off. That got to me. I was a sucker for that, such as it is. I also knew I could live the reality of it — which is something completely fucking different. The romance bit and the rewards come after the work. It's just work most people can't do.

Naughty boys grow into naughty men and by the time you're a naughty man you're called a criminal, or villain, or gangster. Though most people in the business don't recognise those words, they call it 'work'. Going to work or on a job. It's just one of the few kinds of work you can get caught at!

But if 'villainy' is what everyone else wants to call it, and that's what you decide you're gonna be into, then at least be into it with as much style and class as you can. That's true of whatever you do but *especially* if what you do is what most of the world considers bad. The least you can do then is do it with some style and make it palatable.

A real chap ain't a thug or a bully, he's just a man with a lot of class and because he has an inner confidence about what he's capable of, he never has to show that. Or rarely. Because of the business he's in he's generally got more money than everyone else, so he buys nicer clothes and goes to nicer places.

People brush over the criminal fraternity and think they are all the same and that they can tar everyone with the same brush, but if you walk by a building site you see different people doing different jobs, and probably for their own different reasons. Well, villainy is like that. Criminals are the same as everyone else in that they're just as different.

What people don't understand is this: you don't get addicted to being a criminal or to villainy – you actually get addicted to a certain lifestyle and the money that comes with it. I liked the lifestyle and I didn't know anything else that would fund it. Once you've tasted it you can't go back. That's why I understand addiction very, very well.

After a while, after you've been doing it for a few years, you realise that luck's gonna run out some time and one morning there'll be size 10s kicking the fucking door down. But you get addicted to the wages, and working 9 to 5 just ain't gonna pay you that! No straight jobs gonna earn you twenty grand in twenty seconds once a month, but a bank job would. Or it would in the days you could get away with doing a bank.

Years ago you could stand up in class and say my dad's a villain, my dad's a bank robber. I know it's naughty but it had an air of romance to it. But now every crime is just drug-related you can't stand up and say my dad's a drug dealer. It just ain't the same.

What we've got to deal with today, in the twenty-first century, in that walk of life, is the way the media portray you and what they want to call you. The general public is very brainwashed about crime at the moment. If you don't know anything about it except what you read or what they show you on telly then you don't know anything about it. It's like one camera only shows one angle – and that's what you see.

The authorities have so much say over newspapers and television that you are *not* going to see things as they really are. You don't see it during a war, during the Falklands for example; and you won't see it in what they call the war against crime. It's like in Northern Ireland: they would not portray the British Army as being even slightly wrong; they'd just tell you about the IRA, but I'm afraid there is another side. They do the same with British crime and portray it how they want people to think about it.

When you're kids you play cowboys and Indians thinking it was really simple: the cowboys were the goodies and the Red Indians the baddies. That's the myth. We grow up to learn that it weren't really like that. The so-called goodies didn't all wear white hats, and a lot of them were just murdering toerags. Some of the cowboys would just slaughter Indians and nick their land.

Same deal when you play cops and robbers. It all seems so simple. Goodies against baddies. As you grow up some people don't want this particular myth to be destroyed. So the authorities try to keep a lid on news of good baddies and bad goodies. The trouble is, though, that so we have so many bent copper trials that it's hard to keep a lid on it without using an elephant as a weight.

The public are brainwashed into thinking you're a perpetual villain or criminal, whatever you want to call it, but you're not. That ain't it at all. You've just got addicted to a certain lifestyle and having a fucking good time.

You get in the game, play it, and then find a way out. Hopefully one with less risks and as much or more money.

Anyway, what we've got now with all this book-writing and film-making – all this celebrity status stuff – is the chance of making it off something legit and without the risk of getting nicked. What's the worse thing that can happen – your book gets to only No 2 instead of No 1? – or the drinks run out at your film premiere? Big fucking deal. What problems? Fuck all, really, next to risking getting a twenty stretch.

Today, if you get a decent hit, you get a million quid. So whereas most people in my way of life use a book as a swansong, one of the last things they do, for me it's the opposite. More of a springboard into another world. Most people use the fame game as a way of getting their hands on things they've never had – money, women, respect, all those things. But all the naughty geezers that are now doing their books or films have already had a lifetime of those things! They now just want them without the risk of getting banged up.

I also think that getting your life story out in print is a way of having a stab at immortality. The only thing you've *got* to do is die, but you can kind of live on in a way in the things you leave behind. Through your family, for one thing, and other things like books and films or whatever you're into. In the title pages of the books I've had published I noticed a line that said, 'A catalogue record for this book is available from the British Library'. What this means, apparently, is that the British Library is legally bound to keep a record and copy of the book for ever. So *Stop the Ride I Want to Get Off*, and *Raving Lunacy* and this one, and any others, will be there long after I've fucked off upstairs to claim my cloud and have a good old natter with old Holy Hands.

So as royally pissed off as the Metropolitan Police may be at me making a proper go of this fame game there is absolutely *nothing* they can do about the fact that my books will outlive the whole fucking lot of them! *Ha!* Defeated by time.

One big difference between this fame thing happening to me and it happening to the others is I'm a fair bit younger. So it's easy for the police to believe that men such as Freddie Foreman and Tony Lambrianou have retired 'cos they're in their sixties or seventies; but the Old Bill look at me being only 41 and go '*Fuuuuck orf!*' So I get the upside of the age but the downside of the attention. Not that I'm really moaning. Bring 'em on is what I say.

Every day that I'm out and not in prison is a victory and, in some people's eyes, an advert for making crime look like a career option. Not that I'm actually promoting crime, 'cos I don't, I just tell you what I've done. What I actually do say is that the old world is dead: the old gangster/villainy thing is finished. Fucking extinct. It's all been relegated to myth now. Like knights in armour, cowboys and

Indians, cops and robbers. There is no war of wits with a copper on your case now like there was during the sixties or even seventies – 'Nipper' Read after the Krays and the massive organisation after Bruce Reynolds and the Great Train Robbers for instance. Today you're caught by film, video, computers, trackers, bugs, wiretaps, long-range mics, infra-red cameras, satelite dishes, helicopter tails, surveillance teams, stake-outs, lab technicians, TV appeals; practically everything bar putting an ink pad in a bird's fanny so they can get a print off your dick.

No one can survive a three-year warranty being put on their home – that's a licence to listen to everything you say in your house, your car and on your phone. It's difficult to come up smelling of roses after that, even for the Pope let alone a professional criminal.

Now is the wrong time to be a professional naughty person but the right time to try making a profession from having been one. Shoot me with a camera full of film all day long, baby, 'cos I know from experience it's the least painful kind of getting shot. I don't even mind what angle you take the picture from. I'm one of the few that actually *want* you to get my bad side.

But the one thing that don't change, the one thing I'm still addicted to, is having a fucking good time. As yet, they can't touch you for it.

3 WWW.FUCKYOU.COM

If crime don't pay then how come speed cameras raised £200 million last year? And when these new digital speed cameras come in the police start getting a cut of the money. So what the Old Bill means by 'crime don't pay' is that it don't pay for anyone but them.

Which reminds me, I've got a blinding little tip for you here. Get a little bit of black electrical tape and change one letter on your motor's number plate. Now you can go through as many of those little flashing things as you like, or so I've been told. And as long as you throw the tape away after you've used it and you don't have it in the car, if the police stop you and say did you know about that – you go, 'No!' You ain't got the tape in the car and anyone can mess with the outside of your car without you knowing, so . . . fucking listen to me – it works! Allegedly.

One more tip. The cameras that flash as you approach them, those ones are the dummy ones to scare you. They don't have no film in. The real ones actually go off as you pass and photograph you from the back. So tape the back number plate.

See, it's just a question of choosing the right tactic. Like the bloke who told his mate he'd finally found a way of stopping his grandma sliding down the bannister. His mate says, 'How?' The bloke says, 'I wrapped barbed wire around it.' 'I guess that stopped her then,' his mate says. 'No,' the bloke goes, 'but it fucking slowed her down.'

Like I've said before, now is the wrong time to be a criminal. There's too much high-fucking-tech equipment on you, too many laws bent against you, too many surveillance techniques, and you'd most probably have to be in drugs to make the money.

You'd think it'd be seen as a good move for us lot to be getting out of our old world and into legal stuff like book-writing and film-making, but you still get the authorities and ex-coppers like Sir Paul Condom and John 'window salesman' Stalker moaning about villains writing crime books. Fucking hell, you can't win. It didn't stop Stalker trying to flog security devices and Sir Paul from writing his own book though, and they wouldn't have even *had* careers as supposed 'good guys' if there hadn't been any alleged 'bad guys'. So fuck them. Condom's book ain't bad, as it happens – one of the best I've ever coloured in. I kept within the lines and everything. Wicked dot-to-dots as well . . .

As soon as I saw the way things were going in my line of work I couldn't wait to get out the game and get into the media lark. You can make as much money, or more, but without the risks. Although I did sprain my wrist once doing some of the writing. How's that for danger?

Every man should have the right to make what he wants of his life but it just gets up the police's noses so much to see us doing well out of something they can't fucking nick us for! And then when their kids go out and buy our books . . . that's gonna make PC Daddy well chuffed, ain't it? The geezer's gone into the law and order game and thinks he's a hero to his kid but his son gets off on *Lock, Stock*, gangster rap and *Stop the Ride I Want to Get Off.* Whoops. Pardon me for having a more interesting life than a fucking copper.

See, there's no pension plan in our game and people who live for the moment tend not to stash it away for a rainy day. Any road, come to think of it, how the fuck can you save for a rainy day when you live somewhere as piss wet as England? Just a thought.

Maybe their tactic is to push people back into old ways to try earn a living, then the police can turn round and go, 'See! They can't change their ways . . .'

It ain't no surprise to me how the media's got hold of the naughty men and won't let go. It's a big reality injection, and the media people feed off of that. The fucking realness of it can't be faked or made up, can it? And what people don't know is that there's loads of genuinely funny people who live the life. I know the funniest fuckers in the world, and they know how to live large.

21

So I'm being bombarded by thousands of requests to do things: telly, films, documentaries, voice-overs, modelling. Yeah, I know, *modelling*! What's that for then, Dave, I hear you ask, Marks & Spencer's own new range of knuckledusters? No, actually, clever bollocks, it's for the fashion label called Pink. Real classy clobber it is too. They asked me if I'd wear their shirts for an advertising campaign, and I suggested they should use Fred Foreman and Tony Lambrianou as well. Fred and Tony said they'd do it, but only after I'd explained to them that Pink was the name of the company and they wouldn't actually be *wearing* pink shirts and looking like a couple of gays! As if those two scary-looking fuckers ever could.

One other thing that's going great guns and that I really get a kick out of is doing the 'Audience With Dave Courtney' gigs. World champ dope-dealer Howard Marks was the one that sort of kick-started it for me when I saw him do one of his shows at Hammersmith with Neal O'Brien. With me, even from being a kid, I'd always felt that as soon as I woke up in the morning it was like the theatre curtains going up, or the film director shouting 'Action!' So it weren't no great leap forward for me to do what I do anyway but just do it a few feet higher up on a stage. And I fucking love it.

I've done 'Audience Withs . . .' from Brighton to Glasgow and from New York to Tenerife. Sometimes I'll end up with a couple months of shows booked round the country so it's like going off on tour, like a rock band: 'No Sleep Till Peckham!' I know people in most of the towns and cities I go to so there's always a welcome there, and doing the shows makes you more mates so we just have a ball, mate. Every time, all the time.

I did shows in London, Sheffield, Doncaster, Sunderland and Leeds in the space of three weeks. How it works is that if someone gets the idea they want to stage a show they just ring me and ask and if I want to do it and, you know me by now, am I going to say no? Oh, *stop* it! Bring me to my people. Yeah, take me to bed or lose me for ever.

I talk for an hour or more about me – what a stretch – and then people throw questions at me until we work out which one the local undercover copper is. Don't try and tell me they're not there. If they would go to the trouble of trying to stop some of the shows in the first place – and they have tried that – don't tell me they're not gonna sneak someone in on the night to check it out. I always say, 'If the geezer sat next to you is talking into his lapel, smack him in the mouth!'

When I was planning on doing a show down in Gloucester recently the bloke at the venue got a visit from the local plod trying to get him to call it off. But this geezer is a stand-up bloke and he didn't buckle; he called their bluff and did it anyway, 'cos if the shows are legal, which they are, then it's nothing but a vendetta against me. But I've been through that before when they closed down my legit businesses after I arranged Ronnie Kray's funeral.

I can see their point though, because if I was the police I wouldn't want me going round the country enlightening people as to the dirty tricks of the trade that some of our boys in blue get up to. See, their idea is this — *Freedom of speech for everyone but those who use it*.

Well, fuck them. What I'm doing is, as they put it, 'exercising my right to free speech'; and my tongue is pretty well exercised by now, I can tell you. It could jump out of my mouth and run the London fucking Marathon all by itself — 'And the tongue takes it by a short neck!'

The show in Gloucester turned out to be a peach of a show, as it happens. I was being filmed doing the show and the cameraman, Rob Gomez, was offered a joint of mine by Brendan that I'd passed to him. Now, I don't think Rob's a puff smoker but not wanting to offend he took it, not realising that I roll mine quite strong. I was on stage doing the show and I saw everything from my vantage point.

A few minutes later Rob started going white, then green, then he swayed a bit and bullets of sweat broke out over his face . . . and I was watching him out of one eye and trying not to get distracted. Then finally he keeled over and rocked back into this armchair behind him! Out. No one seemed to notice but me and Brendan, but I just carried on regardless 'cos the camera was set up on a stand anyway! The next thing I know, I look down and a Staffordshire bull terrier's walked on stage and started sniffing my feet! Then it looked up, and fucked off again. Everyone in the audience was wetting themselves. I said, 'Don't panic, but don't trust the Staffordshire – I know undercover Old Bill when I see one. Who, me, paranoid?'

The show I did in Doncaster was a riot . . . but the tear gas sorted that out. No, it was wicked. It was arranged by a couple of fellas who're now good pals of mine, Ben Womack and Paul Conway, and was in this big ballroom with hundreds of people there for a five-course meal followed by the show. There was even a picture of me on the fucking menu, which was fine by me but a lady got carried away and ordered me for dessert! Trouble was she was a bit of a specky moose. I told her that I'd always wanted to make love to a woman wearing glasses. She said, Really? I went, Yeah, would you lend yours to that fit blonde bird over there?

After I did my show a Liverpudlian comedian called Sean Stiles did his act and he was the funniest fucker I've seen in a long time. I've been nicking his jokes ever since. After the show we came out of the hotel to find that Ben had laid on three of the longest white stretch limos you've ever seen, waiting to take us all out to a club. Don't mind if I do. And we did.

The gig in Sheffield was a top one as well. One good thing about doing this and travelling around is that you get to meet some funny bastards. We arrived in Sheffield the night before the show and found ourselves put up in this fucking enormous, posh hotel. On a clear day you could see the car park attendant's cottage! They actually ferried us about between the foyer and the rooms in one of those golf-cart buggies. And the porter at this hotel, fuck me, I *swear* to God, he had the *longest* arms I had ever seen outside of a gorilla house in the zoo. He could scratch his ankles with only a slight dip of the shoulders. And he was tall anyway, a proper Lurch from the Addams Family.

So this rubber-band-armed bastard picks up our bags — he didn't even have to bend down — and then this golf cart comes buzzing round the corner to pick us up! Me and Brendan just looked at each other like, y'know, this *cannot* be real. So there's me, Jen and Brendan being chauffeured by Lurch in a golf buggy around a hotel . . . That's normal, innit? I got the double-dildo out of Jen's bag and started giving the geezer directions with it, pointing the way.

Anyway, we gets up to the room, he brings the bags in and I gave him a tip – don't ever wear T-shirts, bendy arms! No, I tipped him, 'cos he was actually a nice geezer, but then on the way out he just topped it all off by turning round as he closed the door to say, 'Night-night!' What is *that*! Night-night? I don't remember hearing that since I was five years old. And now I'm a 41-year-old geezer with his wife being told 'Night-night' by a hotel porter! Fuck me, that was the cherry on the cake that was. I think he only just stopped short of saying 'sleep tight'.

Actually, I think every good hotel should have a Night-Night Service. If you're feeling a bit lonesome when you're away on business, or whatever, you ring down to the front desk and someone goes to you, 'Night-night, love.'

This lanky geezer was absolute classic, mate. Then next morning another fella came up to the room with breakfast. I was feeling in a playful mood so when he came in I made sure I was laid out on the bed practically naked with just this little dressing gown round me and my legs crossed ever so provocatively. That sight caused him a little fright. I'd ordered fried eggs but nearly got scrambled, but he regained his balance and put the tray down. He wouldn't even *look* at me he was so spooked! I told him to take the money for the breakfast from off the table, knowing that there was three grand in cash just thrown on there with the double-dildo laid on top of it as a paperweight. He very very carefully picked out the right amount and left very quickly. And this was all before we'd even done the show and gone out clubbing afterwards.

So you see, if the authorities think they can try and stop certain fellas from writing and talking about their lives – especially the ones that, like me, have a fucking good time with it – then they can obviously go fuck themselves, and they must have the brains that God gave a duck's arse.

Anyway, ain't the internet a fucking invention and a half?! Sorry to sound five years too late but the only PCs I'd heard of wore blue uniforms and pointy hats. And the only time they crashed was during a car chase. But fuck me if I haven't now got my own websites! The official ones are **www.davecourtney.com** and **ww.davecourtney.org.com**, and you can e-mail me at **dave_courtney@hotmail.com.** I'm a proper twenty-first century cunt now, ain't I?

By the way, what do you get when you cross a PC with a nun? A computer that will never go down on you.

My website is the absolute bollocks, mate. It's designed and run by another top geezer who's now become a good pal of mine, Steve Parnell. He just got in touch with me himself after reading *Stop the*

Ride . . . with the idea and he's made it the best one I've seen. I would say that, wouldn't I, but everyone else says it as well so I know it's not just me. It's got articles, pictures, videos, clips from my new movie *Hell to Pay*, interviews, merchandise, competitions, chat room, message board and . . . what else? . . . practically everything to be honest apart from a 24-hour web-camera in my fucking bathroom. Just to catch me on the bog – logging on. Though if you watched the Channel 5 documentary, *Dave Courtney's Underworld*, you'll have already seen Jen and me in a bubble-bath scene.

We do question and answer sessions on the web as well:

Dave, apart from being arrested what's your worse time in handcuffs?
I've been to some fetish parties, mate. I've seen some things in handcuffs!

If there's ever been one, what's your scariest moment?
Sleeping in the funeral parlour with Ronnie Kray was not a fucking nice experience. Even though he was dead you thought he was gonna jump out and punch you in the fucking head. And whatever the ghost of Ronnie Kray would do . . . you know it would be more than just go '*Oooohhhh!!*'

So sitting next to the box and wondering whether the lid was gonna open was fucking awful.

What you gonna do for the next five years?
Post offices.

What did you think of Lennie McLean?
Lenny was awesome. But to say who was the best fighter between him and Roy Shaw was the closest thing to a draw you'll ever have.

I've actually been in the ring with Lenny for quarter of a round! He knew he'd been in a fight with me, mate, 'cos his hands were fucking sore. I had him worried at one point . . . he thought he'd killed me. And after watching him fight and one time hit a geezer round the head three times with the stool, I suddenly thought . . . yeah, I'm pretty good at darts.

Know any jokes, Dave?
About a million. Here's a quick one. Why did Jesus cross the road? 'Cos he was nailed to the chicken.

If there's anything you could change in society what would it be?
The fact that the police investigate the police. They should be accountable to the people.

Does crime pay?
Ask the geezer that services my Rolls-Royce, 'cos I wouldn't know.

All that 'crime don't pay' bollocks: listen, the truth is this — crime pays until the day you get caught. Know what I mean? And you don't know, until that happens, and until you get a guilty verdict and get time — until then you don't know whether it's been worth it or not. For instance, if you've been at the game for only six months and then get nabbed for something that gets you a ten stretch, I'd say you're already pretty fucking well lagging behind.

Hello, Dave. What other books are you going to do?
I'm doing a pop-up dot-to-dot colouring book for kids on the history of the knuckleduster. Available in all good bookshops, and some crap ones as well.

OK, I've already done *Stop the Ride . . .*, *Raving Lunacy* and I've got book number three coming out at Christmas. After that the next one will be the big one, the proper follow-up to *Stop the Ride I Want to Get Off* and it'll probably be called *The Ride Goes On*. Makes sense. And my Jennifer's doing a book about women who used to be married to policemen, and in this book they tell the truth about police dirty tricks.

What's the most bizarre place you've ever ended up?

I spent a day and a half in a broken-down submarine at the bottom of the English Channel. It was down to the Berlin wall coming down. They retrenched thousands of KGB agents, sold off all the tanks and submarines. Someone I knew bought one. We took it for a test drive and the thing broke down. We had to get hold of the coastguard who got in contact with a Russian ex-captain who used to have one.

If you could be anywhere in the world right now where would you be?

In bed with my missus.

It's a bit freaky to think that my web stuff goes out all over the world for people who want it. Even little Japanese kids going on the web: 'Aahh, Dave Courney flom Rondon, Engrand!' You think I'm joking but *Stop the Ride* ... was very big in Japan. For some reason they've really got into the British crime scene thing in a big way. A Japanese writer and photographer even flew over here to do a ten-page piece on me for Japanese *GQ* magazine. Then Virgin sent me a copy of the Japanese version of *Stop the Ride* ... and even though it was a hardback copy it was tiny, about the size of one of our paperbacks. They've got much smaller hands, you see. Weird as well seeing it all written out in Japanese characters. I wondered how they translated something like, 'Leave it out, you silly cunt!

You're doing my head in!' What the fuck is the Japanese version of that?

I'm gonna have something painted down the side of the Rolls, like Del Boy used to have on his van, but mine'll say 'Plumstead, Tokyo, Wormwood Scrubs'. I know that when I visit Japan it'll be the one place that I won't hear one of the things that's always said to me: 'Oh, you're not as tall as I thought you'd be.' Fucking annoying that is. Especially when it's said to me by some shortarse, as it usually is!

It's like when you go to Thailand, a normal-size Western geezer is like a giant to them, so anyone a little bit bigger is like a fucking God. I know a body-builder bloke called Clint Dyer who used to work for me who went to live out there and they just thought he was The Incredible fucking Hulk come to life.

Those tiny Thai birds don't half flatter you, though. Just by comparison you look like a massive-dicked porn star. And if you really want to give your ego a boost, do this – don't take condoms out with you, and wait and buy them out there. It feels so fucking good to walk into the Thai version of Boots chemist and ask for a three-pack of extra large! Bring a few packs back with 'XXL' on the packet, just to leave casually about your flat.

You can get those Thai mail-order brides on the internet now. The postage must be fucking horrendous.

I'm absolutely loving it at the moment, my life. I'm having a ball. If I was made of chocolate I'd fucking eat myself, I tell you. I don't understand those people who strive for attention and fame and then go all sniffy about having their picture taken. Fucking hell, mate, what's that about? Talk to the hand 'cos the head ain't listening, y'know what I'm saying. Most people are really surprised when they get through to me to ask for an interview and I go yeah, straightaway. Even to the little studenty magazines. It ain't exactly hard work is it, me talking about me; and if you've put yourself up for it like I have, how can you not do it?

So they usually begin by being surprised I've said yes, then shocked when I invite them up to my house, and then fucking flabbergasted when they get there and find a *castle*. A triple whammy – and you're very welcome. I was thinking of putting a revolving door on the front of my house but I didn't want it setting off local speed cameras.

Not until I'd got out the black electrical tape anyway . . .

4 GANGSTARS

Right from when I kicked in my first 'emergency exit' door and got me and my mates into the cinema for free I've loved going to the pictures. That was during the days when you could still smoke in there as well. Anybody old enough to remember that time always remembers the beam of light being full of swirling smoke. (Ask your dad!) And if you ever went to the pictures in south-east London and got sat in front of a cocky 13-year-old with his feet on the seat, smoking a cigar, chatting away and twanging some bird's knicker elastic ... *sorry*. But at least I didn't rustle sweet wrappers.

Or leave a mobile phone on. Fuck me. Russell Crowe's just about to decapitate some poor cunt in *Gladiator* and suddenly you hear a fucking ring-tone! You half expect Maximus to pull a Nokia out of his body armour – 'Sorry, babe, can't talk now, I'm in the middle of fighting for my life in the arena. Yeah, I'll get a stuck pig and some new sandals on the way home ...' They were very advanced those Romans, weren't they? But not that advanced.

In fact, in a way, the old door-kicking routine is one that I'm still using today. Every time I meet film producers or go over to America to talk to someone about filming my books, I also think of it as a way of getting all my mates cast in the films as well. Only this time, instead of kicking in the door for them to *watch* films, I'm taking them in with me and actually getting them *in* films.

Anyway, every man loves a good gangster film. None more than me. If you can ignore the fact that most of them ain't accurate depictions of criminal life. I mean, Phil Collins playing Great Train Robber Buster Edwards in the film *Buster*? Do me a favour. They'll be casting two pop singers as the Kray twins next. Oops. Yeah, I know it happened! In *The Krays* the Kemp brothers from Spandau Ballet, Martin and Gary, played Reg and Ron. They weren't half bad, as it happens, for a couple of pop stars. Though I know that both Reg and Ron weren't too happy with the final film. Maybe they wanted it to have a happy ending.

Not many people know (that's my Michael Caine impression) that as well as films taking inspiration from real-life gangsters, sometimes gangsters have taken from the films. Like in the thirties and forties real gangsters actually got more 'gangstery' after they'd seen themselves portrayed in films by Jimmy Cagney and Edward G. Robinson. And after the success of *The Godfather* films American mob guys started being more like they were shown on film 'cos they liked how it looked. Fucking weird one that, innit? Talk about life imitating art.

And talking about talking about life imitating art . . . Guy Ritchie's film *Lock, Stock and Two Smoking Barrels* came out in 1998, just before my first book *Stop the Ride I Want to Get Off*. Vinnie Jones played debt collector Big Chris and acted out some of my life stories. Like I've always said, Vinnie has to act his little socks off playing a hard man 'cos that's always gonna be a big stretch for any footballer. Being known as something like 'the hard man of football' is sort of a backhanded compliment anyway, ain't it? Bit like being known as the toughest vicar in church.

The famous scene where Big Chris takes his young son on a debt collection and threatens a geezer under a sunbed was well known as something I'd done years earlier in my debt-collecting days. It was at a south London gym in Peckham. I'd taken my boy Beau along with me that day, and so he became a little part of history too. In fact when Beau was a boy I had a little doorman-style dinner suit made for him and sometimes I'd take him to work with me! He looked liked the hardest fucking midget in town.

There's always been this relationship between the criminal world and show business. Starting from criminal connections to club-land. That's where it began. Naughty geezers have always liked showing out and showing off; with their clothes, their cars, their ladies. No better place to do that than in a club. It's a small step from there into the worlds of music and film.

Actors have always liked knocking around with the real thing and being on the fringes of naughty people; they get a buzz out of it. And naughty people like the celebrity friends so some of that fame can rub off on them. My theory is that a lot of actors like to mingle with the real thing to pick up some reality. But, at the end of the day, it's not their world. And, remember this, if you haven't grown up within a certain world you can only ever be a tourist there. Don't ever mistake yourself for a native. You'll only get put in the pot and eaten.

Naughty chaps don't really give a fuck for famous people in the way that they're not impressed by all that nonsense. Filming is just all make-believe and playing around really. When you've lived a life that's been the opposite of that in many ways, like you've seen a lot of the extremes of life and risked a lot, then you see the make-believe stuff for what it is. Real boxers all think *Rocky* is rubbish, although still very entertaining, and real villains think that most gangster films are the same.

A lot of the stars that I've met and seen have always been far more impressed by the naughty chaps they've met than the other way around. And rightly so.

That's why when someone who's had more of a proper life gets into acting they don't get all dramatic and start throwing fits over their sandwiches not being cut in half or the sky being the wrong fucking colour, or some such bollocks. One of my favourite actors was Robert Mitchum. Now *he'd* had a life, been nicked and been put on a chain gang, that kinda thing, before he sort of fell into acting almost by accident. There's a story about a young actor fretting about what his 'motivation' for the next scene was. So he asked Robert Mitchum and Mitchum went, 'Your motivation, son, is Friday. 'Cos that's when we get paid.' Top line.

Lee Marvin, he was another of what I call Proper Stars 'cos he was a real man to begin with. Nearly got his arse shot off in the war, got a medal, and then he fought, fucked, drank and had a good time for the rest of his life. *The Dirty Dozen* is one of his films, check it out.

The only pin-up I ever had was Jane Fonda. She starred in that sexy science fiction movie *Barbarella*, wearing all these skimpy little outfits. You only had to take one look at Jane's arse to think, Beam me up, Scotty! I saw that film on TV the other week and it's still a horny little picture, even by today's standards.

Yeah, I had many a wank over Jane Fonda. She was also in a cowboy film called *Cat Ballou* with Lee Marvin. In fact, in the bath the other day, I even had a wank over Lee Marvin. I couldn't believe it! Right film, wrong actor!

Actually, tell a lie, I did have another pin-up: the actress Diana Rigg. She was in the James Bond film *On Her Majesty's Secret Service* and in the TV series *The Avengers*, usually wearing a black leather catsuit. She was proper hot posh-totty, mate, and I had to stay sat on the settee a good half hour after watching *The Avengers*. One day at home when I was a kid, I was flicking through the catalogue that we always got just before Christmas, and I saw the bra and knicker page with Diana Rigg on it! I couldn't believe it. Touch. And I did. I got some scissors and cut Diana Rigg's pictures out of the pages, in all her glory. Trouble was that when my mum saw the catalogue she thought my dad had done it — he copped it big-style when he got home from work! He got called every pervert under the sun. He never knew what hit him — until he regained consciousness and saw it'd been my mum.

If you have any heroes they should at least be real people who've done real things, not people who just play at being real people. Most of the blokes that I held in high esteem when I started out were, in my eyes, the top chaps in London. Guys who I used to see when I was younger and training at the boxing gym: people like Joey Pyle, Freddie Foreman, Roy Shaw, Charlie Kray. Boxers themselves I have a lot of time for. That ain't an easy way to make a living and you've got to have balls and discipline.

One of my boxing heroes was Roberto Duran, the great middleweight champion. Years ago when he was over here doing some charity thing, some boxing demonstration, he actually came to the Thomas à Becket gym. You could pay to spar with him, so I did that, for two rounds. He was in his forties then, and 'cos of the age of his face he looked old, but his body wasn't old and he was still fucking hard as iron. They used to say about him that he had no knees because he didn't know how to back off. He actually made a comeback not long after his trip to London – and at his age.

As for being impressed by so-called 'stars' though, that don't really happen. See, a lot of villains and naughty geezers – especially the older ones from back then – actually lived a kind of 'starry' life already. They got the respect, money, birds, excitement, cars, drugs (optional), no queuing for clubs, freebies, best seats in the house, etc. – the same star benefits that people now get for being famous at something like acting. You know, these geezers were famous in their own communities and most of them rarely left their own stamping ground so they always had that reaction.

At one time the traffic was all pretty one-way: actors and musicians wanting to get into the world of villains but no self-respecting naughty geezer would try to go the other way into films. That's changed now though. Even Lenny McLean, who was the most unactorly, non-poncey geezer you could ever ever meet, got into the old acting game in *Lock, Stock*.

Now it can be a very clever way out of your old crime life and a way of actually making more money from acting out a bank job than actually doing a real one! With none of the risk of getting banged up for a fucking ten stretch. Worse thing that can happen on a film set is that you scare the make-up girl, fluff your lines, or fart and fuck up a take. Hardly life-threatening is it.

I even did a bit in the film *The Krays* playing a real life character called John 'Mad Dog' Mangan. Funnily enough, I'd actually met Johnny before that in Brixton nick (Lenny McLean was also in there on remand for a murder charge he was later found innocent of). We met in the hospital wing when I was in pretending to be ill for something or other. Might have been the fact that the hospital was the only place where you could get a shag.

Anyway, I was in on remand for a charge down to something that happened at a place where I was working called Junction 13. I wasn't touched for it until four months later when some of the people involved saw me on TV and recognised me! Grassed up by a camera! (That's when the BBC made a documentary about me; *Bermondsey Boy*.) I was still living in Peckham then.

Mad Dog had been a member of the Kray twin firm. He was a little geezer but he had a big heart; and it must've been well fucking hidden inside his body 'cos he'd once got shot nine times and lived to tell the tale. Though he nearly died of lead poisoning.

He could do a hundred one-arm press-ups. And he was always singing. Frank Sinatra songs, really loudly and badly. You couldn't help but love him. Especially if you were deaf. We met in the hospital wing at Brixton. So I was play-acting at being ill and Mad Dog had a dicky ticker. He knew I was putting it on but he used to look out for me in there. Even at his age and health he'd be looking out for you!

Anyway, later on, when I'd moved to Woolwich, he came round the flat after he'd done an armed robbery. He was sixty-fucking-nine years of age! He was actually in his pyjamas when he arrived at the flat 'cos he'd already been nicked for the robbery and put in the Brook Hospital. Then he'd had another heart attack and they fucking jump-started him with the electric shock thing. Then while he was at another hospital for tests, he came round, looked around and saw there were no screws – and legged it!

He ran to my house and knocked on the door in his pyjamas. Fucking hell. He still had burn marks on his chest from where they'd jump-started him! He was proper buzzing like he was on speed; and he was going, 'They can't kill me!' Then he dropped to the floor . . . and started doing fifty press-ups. I was going 'Oh, *stop* it! You'll kill yourself.' He just wouldn't let up. Then he started singing these old songs, 'Mar*leeene*! . . .'

I just kept him there for a little and looked after him this time. He stayed a while and then said he didn't want to stay any longer 'cos the kids were too noisy. So he went back.

Yeah, John was the original bloke who said to the judge when he got sentenced: 'I don't give a fuck. I've done more porridge than the three bears!' See what I mean? . . . With real star people like that knocking about, who the fuck is gonna look up to some actor? Let's see Arnold Schwarzenegger do a bank job when he's in his sixties and after two heart attacks. *And* find my house in his pyjamas! No chance.

OK, this is where I do my film review section — a bit like Jonathan Ross but with less hair, better suits and no lisp. You won't catch me rolling my Rs. I've even got my own unique rating system, specially developed by some geezer with a computer and too much time on his hands. It's called the Golden Knuckledusters.

0 Dusters — a complete lightweight; *1 Duster* — first punch knock-out; *2 Dusters* — game, bit of a trier; *3 Dusters* — pretty handy; *4*

Dusters — very, very tasty; *5 Dusters* — the absolute nuts, a fucking animal of a movie.

THE GODFATHER 👊👊👊👊👊

Top mafia film. Loads of *real* stars like Marlon Brando, Al Pacino and James Caan, not pretend ones like that twelve-year-old elf Leonardo DiCaprio — personally, I think the sinking of the *Titanic* was a small price to pay for seeing him drown. Anyway, Brando acts his socks off (and it looks like he's put them in his mouth), playing the head of a mob family. Also accurately shows that bent coppers on the take ain't something the Met invented. There's a higher body count here than a foot-and-mouth outbreak and loads of bloody shootings, including one where a geezer carries on chewing his spaghetti *after* he's been shot in the face. Those Italians do love their food. Bleeding marvellous. The god-daddy of all gangster pictures.

Trivia fact: Marlon Brando's now so fat he's been given his own postcode.

SCARFACE 👊👊👊👊👊👊

Abso-fucking-lutely mental movie. You'll notice I've given it six dusters out of five, which don't make a blind bit of sense but I'm 41½ and it's my book. Al Pacino again, playing a totally big-balled Cuban villain called Tony Montana. Tony fights and fucks and shoots and snorts his way to the top, only taking a break to pfuck Michelle Pfeiffer. The final shoot-out is berserk. Little Al with a massive machine gun (his 'little friend'), screaming at his enemies – 'Choo wan a war?! I *give* you a war! Say ello to my liddle fren!!' The *Gone With the Wind* of gangster films. Epic, mate.

Trivia crap: Al Pacino is so short in real life that if you watch him on a 28" screen telly he's actually lifesize.

GET CARTER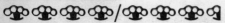

Like plain crisps *Get Carter* is the original and best of the British villain films. Michael Caine plays cool-as-fuck geezer Jack Carter travelling from London to a strange land full of strange-speaking natives – Newcastle – to get revenge for his brother's murder. Loads of top one-liners, classic British motors and Best Supporting Weapon award goes to the good old-fashioned shotgun.

Trivia bollocks: Not a lot of people know this but Michael Caine is actually Chris Evans' dad!

GOODFELLAS/CASINO

Both these mob films are the bollocks with Robert De Niro and Joe Pesci on top form in both. And fuck me, Joe Pesci knows more swear words than I do. His acceleration is wicked — he goes from 0 to 60 'fucks' in about ten seconds. *Goodfellas* is wicked but spoilt by the geezer grassing up his mates at the end. In *Casino* Joe Pesci puts someone's head in a vice. Show these films in a double bill to your granny and watch her have a stroke. (Oh, I see I've given 3½ dusters to *Casino*! Half a duster? That must be a little one for just two fingers.)

Trivia shit: Real-life Mafia guys appear in both films.

RESERVOIR DOGS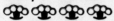

This lot do shout a lot, don't they? Fucking hell. They've got even less volume control than Tom Jones. *Reservoir Foghorns* might be a better title. Good suits and messy shoot-outs, though. I pity the fucker who got the dry-cleaning bill. That'd need another bank job. Bit of a modern classic in gangster films, this one.

Trivia tripe: Quentin Tarantino's real name is Kevin Plank.

LOCK, STOCK AND TWO SMOKING BARRELS

At last. The first decent British crim film for fucking ages. Glad I didn't hold my breath waiting, though; blue skin don't suit me. Wicked film and well funny too, which is unusual. The young lads are a bit lightweight, but then stood next to Lenny McLean that's understandable. In fact, they're lucky not to come off looking like six year olds.

My son Beau got a major flashback watching the famous sunbed scene with the character Big Chris and his son Little Chris. Vinnie Jones shows he can act. Tough one for a footballer. Guy Ritchie is a very good director, *and* his missus is Madonna. Lucky, lucky *bastard*.

GANGSTER No1

Another British gangster movie that didn't get the recognition it deserved. Personally I feel it's at least as good as *Lock, Stock*. Excellent performance by Freddie's son Jamie Foreman playing a geezer who's a ringer for Ronnie Kray. And enough shooters, blood and violence to please everyone.

HELL TO PAY

I just happen to have made my own film recently myself. As you do when there's nothing on telly. It's a full-blown villainous epic, made in England. Starring yours truly. I don't know which we shot more of – film or blanks. The Met's Armed Response Unit got a fair bit of overtime out of us, though, and we scared more innocent bystanders than Cilla Black and Dale Winton doing a joint streak.

Although it's a fictional story – about two brothers in the same firm – it's also got a documentary-style element to it because of the way it's shot and because a lot of people in the film actually do what they are playing: so doormen are played by real doormen, prostitutes are played by prostitutes, nutters by nutters, etc. The only thing we couldn't get are some genuine members of the police 'cos we didn't have enough money for the bribe. We went one better though and got Bill Murray, the actor who played the bent copper in *The Bill*, to play the part of my brother. And excellent he is too.

There's also interesting people appearing in it like the model Jo Guest, Spider from *Coronation Street*, Andy Beckwith, Garry Bushell, John Conteh, Diamond-back Dom, 'Lone Wolf' Dave Legano, Darren Mitchell, Lee Vaselo, Big Mark and Big Nick from Coventry, Mickey Biggs – son of Ronnie, Robbie Williams' dad, Nasty Nick from *Big Brother*, and the other Nasty Nick from *EastEnders* and a lot of the naughty-looking geezers who were in *Lock, Stock* and *Snatch* 'cos they were all my pals anyway.

It is the most realistic gangster film I imagine anyone has ever seen. It's a low budget film but with the favours I pulled to get it made it probably comes out at the equivalent of a £3 million movie. And don't worry, it's got ample violence, loads of tits and bums and all the ingredients that make a proper gangster film – the bare-knuckle boxing match, the gun fights, the sex; but it's more realistic than the others. We had no script as such and improvised and ad-libbed, in the way you have to do when you're actually nicked! Which is why everyone in the film was so good at it.

Trivia: No animals were hurt in the making of this film but half a dozen human beings and three traffic wardens were accidently killed. Sorry.

My biggest, biggest regret about making *Hell To Pay* is that everyone who was in it . . . isn't in it. Meaning that because the film had to be a certain length some people unfortunately ended up being edited out, and I'm gutted about that 'cos they were people who supported me, and the film, came to Cannes, and gave their time and talent as much as anyone else.

I'm glad I didn't have to make the decision 'cos it would've been too hard. Thank fuck we had someone in the editing suite doing that. But heartfelt apologies to anyone who didn't make the final edit.

I tell you, we had a ball making the film and blew up and shot up half of London and Portsmouth in the process.

We worked flat out to get it finished just in time to take it to the Cannes Film Festival. We took a luxury coach full of friends and journalists down to the south of France to the festival in May, with two Harley Davidson outriders and three Mercedes limos accompanying us all the way. It was a fucking blinding sight driving in and out of the Channel Tunnel I can tell you, but it did put the shits up customs officers on the other side.

We drove out looking like a combination of The Wacky Races, the President's motorcade and a bikers' holiday outing all rolled into one! I think they thought it was the advance party for Britain's invasion of France. I had to explain: I said, '*No*. We only look at you as a *snack*, my little French cousins — we've got much bigger fish to fry!'

Yeah. First the world, and then . . . *Disneyland*!

5 DAVE CRACKS THE PHILOSOPHER'S STONE

I found this massive book of quotations at home propping up my house. Must be why they say wisdom is the foundation. Anyway, as it happens, some of them got it wrong.

Chairman Mao – 'The journey of a thousand miles begins with a single step . . .'

'. . . or however many it takes to get to the car' – Dave

Anon – 'There are no sadder words than: if only . . .'

'. . . except: you're nicked' – Dave

Walt Disney – 'If you can dream it, you can do it . . .'

'. . . unless you dream of fucking Minnie Mouse' – Dave

'Consider this: what would you attempt to do if you knew you could not fail?

'. . . I'd attempt to do Madonna, with Jen' – Dave

F.D. Roosevelt – 'There is nothing to fear but fear itself ...'

'... and your missus with the hump!' – Dave

W.B. Yeats – 'Tread softly because you tread on my dreams ...'

'... but I've got witnesses to say I was miles away' – Dave

Earl Nightingale – 'Change your thinking and you change your life ...'

'... change your socks and you keep your friends' – Dave

F.E. Smith – 'The meek shall inherit the earth ...'

'... but only when the strong tell them they can' – Dave

Metropolitan Police – 'Crime doesn't pay ...'

'... no comment' – Dave

6 A CHAT WITH CHARLIE

Me and Charles Bronson didn't get off to the best of starts, which was strange for me because I usually get on well with most of the tattooed, shaven-headed, heavily muscled, big-bearded, hostage-taking, maximum-security, infamous and certified criminals that I meet!

That was the reason there, really – that me and Charlie *didn't* actually meet: we'd just heard about each other. And 'just hearing' can lead to wrong impressions. Sometimes you do really need a face-to-face.

It was when I got slammed in Belmarsh A-Cat on remand for an up-and-coming trial. Charlie was already in there of course. He heard through the screws that I'd handed in two Rolexes to property and he had me down as a flash bastard. Which, as I admit myself, ain't far from the truth *but*, as my calling card says, 'Dave Courtney – a flash bastard but a *nice* flash bastard'.

Anyway, our little misunderstanding sorted itself out and me and Chas became pals. When I got a 'not guilty' and got out I started visiting him and still do. I also arranged the wedding reception after he recently got wed inside to his lady, Sara.

He sends me some of his famous drawings, which I pin up on the fridge to scare the kids away from my apple-pie stash.

Charlie is famous for being rated as Britain's most dangerous prisoner. Can't think why. Might be something to do with his habit of taking guards and other prisoners hostage, and then taking them for walkies up on the roof. He's been on more roofs than Santa Claus. He's in *The Guinness Book of World Records* too is old Charles — most sit-ups, longest time in solitary, most rooftop protests . . . maddest beard.

This is an interview I did with him by phone for *Front* magazine:

Charles, how are you, mate?
I'm all right, Dave. I'm up in Hull now and I'm doing 3,750 press-ups a day.

I ain't gonna challenge you. What would you say if God tried to enter your life?
I'd say, 'Would you like to share an apple pie with me?'

Can you blame any incident in your childhood for the way you turned out?
No, I had a lovely mum and dad, it was just the teachers beating me all the time.

Do you feel guilty about anything?
No. The only sadness in my life is upsetting my mother. She's still alive and still going strong. Apart from that, I don't regret anything.

Right. Tell us how you came to be called after Charles Bronson, the actor who starred in the *Death Wish* films.
When I done my unlicensed boxing, Paul Edmonds, my fight manager, said to me 'Charlie' – well, my name was Mickey Peterson then – he said, 'Do a bit of boxing, unlicensed, but box under an alias.' He decided on Charles Bronson and then when I got nicked they fucking charged me as Charles Bronson and it's been with me ever since. It's unbelievable, I don't know anything about Charles fucking Bronson. People say I idolise him, but I ain't even seen the telly in twenty years. How the hell do I know about Charles Bronson?

Twenty years?
Well, out of 25 years in prison I have spent 22½ years in isolation. In solitary confinement; behind the door.

What makes you laugh?
I love having my toes being tickled. I once got the Iraqis to tickle them.

How the hell did you manage that?

There was eight of them and they'd hijacked a plane from Iraq to Stansted Airport. Now this was a bunch of filthy terrorists, walking round prison like jack-the-lad. Anyway, I had a scrap with one of them and then the next day I was on my way to breakfast and they put a fucking noose round my neck and pulled me into their cell. They actually took me hostage – the cheek of it. As I was dragged into the cell I saw this big pot of vaseline and thought they were gonna try and do me so I fought for my life. Five of them ran out of the cell, so I tied the other three of them up and after a little while I got one of them to tickle my toes to liven things up a bit.

And when you took them hostage, all that stuff about your terms – the sandwiches, helicopter, and all that . . . is that really what you asked for?

Yeah, that's true. I don't deny that. But you must remember, I had ten hostages, Dave. Which must have been a world record.

How do they treat you in Hull?

Very fair. In some prisons I'm trapped like a mad dog. But that's mostly in the local dungeons. I'm fed under a door; I'm chained up to go out in the exercise yard and chained up to come back. But when I come to these units, they give me a little bit of respect and a bit of space.

What are the best and worse prisons then?

The worst one I ever done was Rampton, when I was certified mad back in 1977. That was bad. And I mean cold baths, drugging me up and everything. That was a bad place. But the best one I ever done bird in has to be Ashworth maximum security hospital in Liverpool. But now they've got that fucking Ian Brady geezer [the Moors Murderer] up there, I can't do the bird there now – I can't do bird with people like that.

You're the original rooftop protester. Which one's your favourite?

Well, I done Liverpool's once, and Parkhurst's once. But me favourite roof's got to be Broadmoor. I done that three times – that was my hat-trick.

Tell me a secret.

Well, I'm in love with apple pie, and once I've eaten that apple pie . . . I'll have another one.

So you love a bit of twos-up with a tart – don't we all! What about this fighting lark?

Throughout my stretch I've had only 69 days of freedom and it was during that brief spell I had the three fights and won them all.

Right, listen, have you got a softer side?
Well, I do like poetry to a degree. As long as it doesn't go on about flowers and trees and has a bit of body to it. It comes to me in my sleep, my poetry.

As this is coming out at Christmas, I want a Christmas message for our readers. Anything . . . I wish you could sing.
Course I can fucking sing. (*For the next two minutes solid Charles sings his version of Louis Armstrong's 'Wonderful World'.*)

Totally wicked! Now tell me, what do the psychiatrists say about you?
Well, when I arrived at Broadmoor in 1977 I was told by the doctor, 'We only ever take the best here, Charlie, and you're the best.'

Do you reckon you're mad, Charles?
I don't think I'm mad but I do think the system has made me a bit disturbed. Yeah, a little bit disturbed.

Does the full moon affect you?
I suppose it has done in the past, especially since I've had this beard. It's almost down to my belly button now but it's coming off January 1. I had a laugh the other day, I got a piece of string, wrapped it round my beard, and picked up a washing machine with

my beard. I had four cons watching and it nearly tore me fucking face off, but I picked it up all right.

Talking of hair, who's your barber?
Well, I shave my own head, I have done for twenty years. I've got me own razor, a Gillette Sensor. Oh yeah! A lovely razor that is.

Is there anything you need, Charles? D'you want me to send you some phonecards or something?
I'm sweet as a nut, mate – I don't need nothing.

There must be something?
Well, I'd just like to say that I love my mother very much, and I miss her dearly, and she loves me. And I miss all my good friends and I love them and respect them dearly. The enemies, I miss them too. Always will. Oh, and give my mate Paul a nice mention. He's a lovely fella, Dave – he does a lot for me.

Listen, you're not a police-hater, are you?
To be honest, I don't fucking hate anybody. I respect any man if he does his job properly. Whether he's a screw, a guvnor, a copper or a judge. If he does his job proper and fair, who am I to slag him?

How old do you feel?
I feel 23.

Oh, stop it, you flash bastard.
Honest, that's how old I feel. I don't drink, I don't smoke, I have no sex, I have a routine in my life, I have a regular diet, plenty of sleep – I feel fantastic.

How long before they let you out?
I reckon if I get parole I could be out in two years, but at worst I'll be out in five and a half.

D'you have a message for everybody?
What I say is this: Do what you want to do, but just make sure you can sleep in peace at night. And if possible stay away from drugs – drugs are filth. I can't understand people putting stuff up their noses and in their veins, you know; why kill yourself?

Listen, Chas, I'm sorry about the shitty start between you and me.
Aw, listen, forget it – that's all behind us now. I tell you, I loved that section in *Front*, with all those tits. But I'll tell you what, when it's my turn, I want apple pies. God bless and happy Christmas, everyone.

And the same to you, Chas. The same to you.
I think you're the absolute bollocks, Charlie – let 'em have it!

7 MAD, BAD AND HILARIOUS TO KNOW

You do any job for twenty years and you make mistakes; any job, even like mine was, debt collecting. It's real black comedy stuff sometimes. I've booted in the wrong door loads of times and then it's, 'Oh . . . next door, is he? Cheers.' Then you'd kick in that door and end up skating on it like a surfboard down the hallway, running over the cat.

But because you're doing something some people see as bad you have to keep it polite and classy. So I'd always leave behind more than enough money for a new one with the person whose door we'd mistakenly booted in.

You meet the funniest people too. In both senses of the word. Good description of my mates, that title — mad, bad and hilarious to know.

When you live in this circle it's just fun, and normal. Things like staying up till 6 am, clubbing till Wednesday, not coming home 'til January, guns in the house, knuckle-dusters on the table, cash in the fruit bowl, different car every month, parking and speeding ticket bonfires, choice of knock-off gear, mates getting sent down/doing bird/coming out, people sometimes getting shot, no queuing, fights on the door, and the best shoes.

And all this over one weekend!

It was unreal. Completely mad. It sounds all wild and mad, and it is, but not so mad to us that were living it. Sometimes a regular nine to fiver would drop into our world, you'd take them out, show them a bit of it, and they'd totally freak. Then you'd think, Oops! bit of a mistake there, better not take them out again. Showed a bit too much, a bit too soon. Most people got to ease into our world gently, like someone landing on another planet.

I got paid once to blow up a car. Then I rang the guy up and said it's done. He said, No, I've just seen it driving around. Fuck me, I'd only gone and done the wrong car. 'Cos some poor fucker had the same car in the same area. Except it was now in a different area. On its roof. With the wheels in four different postcodes. How the fuck did I know they made all Cortina 1600 Es in gold with black vinyl roofs? I blamed Ford.

There used to be a club called Twilights in Sydenham and by the bus stop across the road was one of those electricity cupboards. Behind it the local lollipop lady used to hide her sign and jacket. I can't remember how I knew they was there. I must've seen her put them there once. Anyway, one morning when we'd all come out the club, it was too good to resist, so I ended up in a fluorescent bib and with a giant fucking lollipop, stopping early morning traffic and waving twenty flat-nosed geezers across the zebra crossing. Then they turned round and walked right back across again. Oh, those early-morning commuters were so amused! Did feel a bit bad about holding up the ambulance, though. And the hearse. And the fire engine.

We used to have this big house that all the doormen rented. If loads of you chipped in with a bit you could afford to get a massive place. We all crashed there at weekends and nights. And crashed cars into the garden. You've never seen such a fucked-up carpet in your life. It had been dusted with more powders, impregnated with more spunk and burnt with more fags than a coke-high whore into S&M.

This one time we all went back to the house, and then at nine o'clock one of our number had to go, but he was one of the key holders. He was a weekend dad, though, and he took his kids swimming on Sundays. So we all went with him. Fifteen doormen – and all with the legs cut off our trousers at the knee: our version of 'trunks' – all went swimming at nine on a Sunday morning in Forest Hill Swimming Baths, after working all night at a club. It was ever so slightly mental and dropping into the deep end was a fucking good wake-up call!

I bought some live eels from the winkle stall outside the baths. I wrapped them in a towel and then flipped them in the pool water as I walked past. I was expecting mass panic and some 87 year old breaking the 100-metres record ... but nothing. Not a peep for twenty minutes. Not until this dopey, specky bastard saw one. He had these massive thick lenses on that were so thick they must've magnified everything five times bigger. Well, he saw an eel and started pointing them out to everyone. Which helped. Everybody began screaming. Then Specky started shouting that they were coming out the drains! Which helped even more. These black eels were wriggling about everywhere.

So they evacuated everyone out the pool — DON'T panic! Everyone OUT! — and then drained the water. We all queued up for our 75p rebate 'cos we'd had to leave early; and looking at the queue — 6 kids, 4 mums, 3 grannies, 1 specky prat and 15 giggling nutters in cut-off dinner suits — it didn't take Sherlock Holmes to work out who the Phantom Eel Chuckers were.

Going back to when I used to work on the dust, there was this geezer there who was a condom short of a three-pack. He was always nicking animals, exotic animals, like llamas and lizards and spider monkeys and fuck knows what else. He probably had the last dodo. He used to fake death certificates for them and keep them. In the end he got nicked for it and ended up on the telly! Anyway, I got into him 'cos I knew there'd be something I could get from him at some point. And there was — a couple of crocodiles.

They were only little things. One died, and the other fucker just grew and grew and grew. It was eating me out of house and home. In fact, it did start eating the house. I had to get rid of it and the RSPCA just weren't 'aving it, y'know what I mean.

So I let it go in Dulwich Park boat pond and it spent all summer eating ducks, chewing oars, biting boats, scaring kids and appearing in news stories in the local paper! True. It became like a Loch Ness monster type thing – does it or doesn't it exist? Winter proved that it did exist 'cos the fucker died of cold and its bloated body bobbed up to the surface. So it was proved to be real not myth.

One time me and Big Marcus went on a debt collection to Middlesbrough College, of all places. Three and a half-hour fucking drive to get there. It was one of them oh-that-don't-sound-too-far jobs. By the time you finally get off the motorway you need to shave your head again. We just ended up driving and driving. Then when we got there this geezer wasn't even at home! I knew he went to this college nearby so we went in. All the little students were around and us two walked in looking like we'd specifically gone in to kill someone or something. I'm in my I'm-gonna-kick-your-head-in clothes, and Marcus is in all black looking like . . . well, looking like *Marcus*! We looked like we *ATE* vegetarians and went on dolphin-killing holidays. There were all these kids about, just . . . staring. I thought, Oh, not a good idea. Just being told about us being there probably made him run out to the bank. You can't beat a bit of advance publicity to lay the groundwork.

Me and Ian Tucker had this debt collection once. We went to go and wake up this geezer in a farmhouse one night. Fear works like this . . . it breeds on the unknown. So waking up and finding two strange geezers stood next to your bed looking down on you like me and Tucker, knuckle-dusters glinting in the moonlight, that's definitely gonna get your attention, y'know what I mean? We obviously ain't there to give you a foot massage. Not a gentle one anyway. And if this kind of coup happens when it's dark then it's even better.

All that would have worked *if* the bloke hadn't heard us creeping up the stairs — and *fuck* me those stairs were so bloody noisy — 'cos old houses do make a racket at night, don't they? Anyway, this geezer comes out with a shotgun and lets a case off at us. We've just got a duster each for defence so we jumped right over the bannister and started running about for the exit; but we couldn't find the fucking door, and the bloke's coming down screaming and shouting. All of a sudden Tucker got the right hump 'cos he couldn't find the door and he just started running back up the stairs straight at this geezer! The bloke shat himself, dropped the gun and ran back into his room. I couldn't fucking believe it — and neither could he, obviously. But once old Tucker's got the bit in his teeth he's like the devil himself, actual horns come out. He's even got three sixes tattooed on his body. The devil himself.

Another mate of mine who definitely, *definitely* has his moments of satanic possession is Mad Pete. The famous Mad Peter (or famous now that he's been in all my books!) There's only one Pete, thank fuck: because if there was two I wouldn't like to be in the room when they had a row.

When we were all sat round the table at my house once, Pete came out with the funniest line. He was telling some tale about the usual madness and he obviously wanted to get on to another point so he said, 'Anyway, after I was hit with the machete . . .' and went on to something else! We all went, Whoa, hold it! Hang on, Pete! Back up to the machete bit!

Turns out he'd had a row with four geezers – which is usually just about fair odds where Pete's concerned – but ended up getting proper chopped to the head and shoulders by one of them with a fucking machete. Pete was up and about a few days later. But you know that a bloke's had some mental times when he can come out with a casual 'anyway after I was hit by the machete'-type line.

Better than that, Pete once had an 80-mile car chase across Spain being shot at by loads of police cars. He crashed through barriers, drove through fields, and did a real *Gone In 60 Seconds*. They were shooting at him, he was firing back. *And*, the very best bit, HE GOT AWAY! Go, Pete! When you saw the photographs in the newspaper of his car it was like a fucking teabag, you've never seen so many holes in your life. There wasn't a window or light left, all four tyres gone, and Pete actually got out of it alive and ran away. He never had a thing wrong with him. He's just one of those people who, even though he does mental things, always seems to be protected, like he's got a light around him.

Usually a blue flashing one, as it happens.

This bloke walked into my pub the other day and asked me the quickest way to Charlton. I said, 'Are you walking or driving?' He said he was driving. I said, 'Yeah, that's definitely the quickest way.' Silly git.

Me and Jen were on this train once and there was this big, fat geezer, this ticket inspector, giving us real grief. Then Jen said, 'You can say what you like to me but I know you can't wipe your bum properly . . .' And that just silenced him, he did *not* know what to say to that. He really wasn't expecting it, and neither was I — I just couldn't stop laughing.

Herbie was a mate of mine who couldn't stop laughing. He was a bloody good laugher and a really good audience, was Herbie. I had a BMW workshop and parts shop with him. This is going back loads of years now. Practically every part in this BMW part shop was nicked. One day I got a brand new 7 series, top of the range it was; 30 grand's worth of car. Just after I'd driven it into the workshop the carphone rang and I answered it.

There was this really panicky-sounding geezer on the other end. He said he'd only just picked it up and he didn't mind if we drove around in it as long as we left it in one piece. I gave him the bad news; that as I was looking at it, the only part still left in one piece and working . . . was this phone.

Honestly, sometimes it's so sad to hear a grown man crying. Down a phone.

The local plod eventually got wind of the operation and paid the place a visit one day. I used to have a secret room there upstairs where I took birds. It was hid behind a false bookcase. Herbie was out the front in the shop but I could hear everything. Now Herbie ain't the slipperiest thing when it comes to serious questioning. The two coppers pointed to all the parts and asked where they came from. Herbie said he didn't know. They asked who his partner was and Herbie said, 'I don't know. I just know him as "Dodgy Dave".' Oh, nothing suspicious there then, Sarge. I think the word 'dodgy' did it for me.

So, anyway, the Old Bill left a message and I had to go down the station to avoid a return visit and a raid. When I got there the copper was half smiling. He went, Oh, you must be 'Dodgy Dave', then! He said they knew what was going on but I could tell he didn't want to waste his time busting us. So he said, 'Just show us *one* receipt for *one* genuinely bought part. Just one in the whole place . . .!' Fucking hell, I thought, start with the easy ones first! I couldn't find even a nut and bolt that hadn't been lifted. Anything that wasn't nailed down we took; and even if it was nailed down we took it. And the nails it'd been nailed down with. All we left were the nail holes.

About this time I drove down to Maidenhead in a red BMW of mine for a punch-up for a bloke called Chris, who was John Boy's associate. They was a lot of camaraderie in those days, and if you helped other people out, they helped you. And you wanted to do that and build up a kind of army you could call on if needs be. So we went down there for this Chris, with two brothers, Italian Tony and his brother Louie. Oh, and Fat John. It went off big time and I got my fucking head kicked in again. So, lucky that time!

Now, as you might guess, I ain't the best at keeping under the speed limit. And that's just when I'm in a club. But every time I drive into London so many speed camera flashes go off it's like being followed by a pack of paparazzi! Honestly, sometimes I feel like Princess Diana driving through Paris! By the way, weren't that little incident a bit iffy?

One day I'm gonna get all the images of me from the speed cameras, splice them together and enter it in the Best Short Film category at the Oscars. No, come to think of it, forget the 'short' bit – it'll be a full length epic up there with *Gone With the Wind*: I'll call it *There Goes a Rolls!*

Little tip here. If you need to get somewhere sharpish and don't want bothering by some troublesome prick of a traffic cop, just deck your car out with white ribbons as if you're a wedding car that's late for the bride. Even some cunt of a copper ain't gonna pull you over. Use it sensibly though, preferably on a big car, and white if possible. It works a treat with my Roller – I've driven off to so many 'weddings' the neighbours think I've become a vicar – but for fuck's sake don't try and carry it off with a poxy Honda hatchback held together by rust and spit. You'll just get everybody pointing. And the wedding trick don't generally work if you're caught at midnight coming out of a pub car park on a Tuesday night. I know.

Mad the things you do when you're younger when you think you'll live for ever. Mind you, I still think I'm going to. I ain't gonna make a Will, I'm making a Won't! I used to have this American muscle car called a Pontiac Firebird Trans-Am. You can tell just from the name it was a fucking beast of a motor. It was blood red with a big V8 lump under the bonnet, chrome wheels and hot-rod tyres. Mopeds used to snap in two just at the sight of it. It used to try and mount red buses from behind 'cos it thought they were fat-arsed mommas!

Driving home one day with some mates, Danny and Ray Bridges, on this quiet bit of motorway, Danny suddenly started wondering out loud if it was possible to climb out one window, go across the roof, and get in the other side. Once he'd started wondering he felt like he had to do it. So we're going along at 100 mph and he got out the one side – it was a pillarless coupé – then swung up and stuck to the roof like a fucking crab. Now what?

His trouser legs were flapping and snapping in the wind like the tails of a kite, and I fucking bet it was cold! 'Getting ups' are always a fuck-load easier than 'getting downs', though, aren't they? You noticed that? Before frostbite kicked in Danny edged over and swung himself legs first in through the other side, behind the driver's seat.

See, we made our own amusements in those days! None of these bleedin' computer games and DVDs for us. We climbed on to car roofs for fucking entertainment we did!

Even before that I had a souped-up Triumph Vitesse. I was sat in it one day when this car went zipping by like a bomb. Someone had nicked it. Then this young copper's head appeared at my window, asking to commandeer my car to chase the other one. I said fuck off. Then he recognised me. It was a mate of mine I'd gone to school with, Damien Solly! He'd only gone on and joined the Old Bill. So he tried again – he went, 'Go on, Dave! Lend us the car. It's me!' I went, 'I don't care, Damien. You can still fuck off!'

When my debt collecting took off big-time after the *Bermondsey Boy* documentary, I made a lot of money and bought a load of cars: a Ford Thunderbird, a hearse, a Mark II Jag, a Rolls, a bubble car, a Cadillac, an E-type Jag.

One time, years later, they really, really pursued me over a speeding offence they'd caught me for. They even let me go to prison on remand in Belmarsh, go to court for that charge, get found not guilty and come out *before* they pounced right back on me and hit me with this stupid speeding thing! This was about nearly two years later! Fucking hell, it'd been so long, what with the remand and the trial, that I think I'd even forgotten *how* to drive.

It was when we were out driving in Southend and someone at the wheel, Mark Riggs, was proper hammering it. And it must have been fucking fast for me to think so. So he pulled up under a bridge and I took over and drove us on. What I didn't know was that he'd gone through two speed guns and been clocked at 137 mph. So when we got pulled over a few minutes later they nicked me for that 'cos I was behind the wheel. Even though we had a carload of witnesses to say I hadn't been driving through the cameras, and Mark himself stood in court and swore it was him that had been driving, they still did me for it.

Really, they just wanted to ban me or get me for anything they could to make life inconvenient after I'd beaten them in court. So the judge found me guilty. I thought, I've got to say something here; so I said, 'Hold it! You're part of the same conspiracy as the rest of them.' He took offence and went, 'Be quiet!'

I went, 'NO! *You* be fucking quiet! I've had to listen to you for three days ...!' The judge said I had to be taken down. So an alarm button was pushed somewhere and court security came in. Court security ... you know, the Brown Uniform Brigade, with the silly hats and white fluffy socks – failed the security job in Sainsbury's 'cos they couldn't be trusted to guard a cabbage.

I said, 'Don't you fucking *dare* try and take me downstairs by your-selves, you silly little cunts!' They didn't know what to do then. Now, the copper that had originally nicked me all that time ago, he had to be there 'cos he was the arresting officer. In the time since he nicked me he's come off the bikes, got a desk job and put on a good four stones. He'd told Jenny that he'd felt like he'd got to know her over the last couple of years; she looked at him and said, yeah, and I feel like I've watched you grow . . . and grow . . . and grow.

I said to the copper, 'I bet that lot make you feel a lot better, don't they?' meaning the security guards. He said to me that he wouldn't try and use the cuffs or restrain me, and he asked if I'd let him lead me down. So I did. And he just held me ever so slightly by the sleeve so he could say that he'd taken me down.

My solicitor came running downstairs, white-faced and freaking out, asking me why I'd done what I'd just done.

I said, 'You wouldn't understand . . .'

He said, 'I want to *try*!'

Anyway, he said unless I apologised they'd hold me there for contempt of court and charge me in the morning, which meant my solicitor had to be there for that, to defend me. But he was supposed to be in the Old Bailey. So he was panicking and he said I had got to apologise. To which my stock answer is — when someone tells me I've *got* to do something — the only thing I've got to do . . . is die. And certainly not apologise.

Eventually he went and did it for me, on my behalf – I said it was OK for him to do that – and he got his day to go off to the Bailey.

Oh yeah, just remembered, something that happened when I came out of the court. This was one of the funniest, most enjoyable little stunts. So, there I am coming out the court fresh from my driving ban and who should be there on the steps but a reporter from the *Sun*. And at the kerb was my Roller. I said, that's more like it, got in, slammed the half-ton door and started her up. The reporter came up to the window, looking puzzled. He went, 'But you're banned. You're not driving off, are you? Oh, I get it . . . you're doing a photo-session!' I said, 'I am most certainly fucking not! I'm going home!' And I drove off laughing, watching him in the rear-view mirror watching us disappear.

There's only two things certain in life: one is that we'll eventually die, and two is that when I go for a night out I will act bloody stupid. During the hearing, when the judge said, 'Is your name Dave Courtney?' I said, 'Yes, it is, but I wish it wasn't today.' He looked at me over his glasses but 'cos I kept a dead straight face he didn't know what to think.

Anyway, there's this lesbian who goes to the gynaecologist's and while he's examining her he says, 'You've got the cleanest vagina

I've ever seen.' The lesbian says, 'Thanks, I've got a woman who comes in twice a week.'

And speaking of cleaners, remember the scene in *Pulp Fiction* where John Travolta accidently blows off the guy's head in the back of the car? What they do then is call in a character who is a 'cleaner', meaning someone who takes care of troublesome things like dead bodies. Well, you don't want them littering up the house. So, one time I got raided at home by the Old Bill: the usual routine — let themselves in with a sledgehammer, redecorate the house with their footprints, do a bit of feng shui with the furniture, turn a thirty-piece dinner set into a thousand-piece one, kick the cat, empty the hoover bag, drag everyone out of bed, play hopscotch on my head, scare the kids, rape the budgie, and generally behave like a bunch of Nazi Avon ladies making Jewish housecalls.

The funniest bit, though — yeah, there *was* actually a funny bit in it all! — was when they saw something written on the kitchen notice board: it said, URGENT CONTACT LENS CLEANER. They went mental over that and started shouting, 'Who's Len's cleaner?! Who is Len's cleaner!' I couldn't fucking believe it. Getting so worked up about a reminder for Jen to get some contact lens cleaner! 'Cos that's all it was. Talk about getting the wrong end of the stick. It was like a violent version of *Only Fools and Horses*. What a bunch of silly plonkers.

Somebody I knew called Dave was one of the first DJs to play garage music in this country when it first came out. He said that everybody was gonna absolutely love it, and he was right. It was slower music than we were used to in clubs, but he got such a buzz from playing it that it was infectious.

Anyway, this other fella I knew, Ray, wanted to get into drug-dealing but he didn't know one end of a drug from the other. So he told this Dave that he was going to buy a couple of thousand Es and asked him to go along and take one to see if they were all right. They went to the buy and Dave opened the packet, took one out the middle, and ten minutes later said that they were OK. Bought them all. Later on, complaints started flooding in from people that Ray had started selling them to. Turns out these 'Es' were actually fish-tank-cleaning tablets! So Ray's now got £7,000 worth of fish-tank water cleaners.

Ray blamed Dave for saying they were OK, went to visit him and ended up dangling him out the window of the highest block of flats in London, the ones beside Guy's Hospital. He was fourteen floors up and looking down.

I happened to be there. It was Ray's thing but I was in the room, but I didn't really want to be because if someone dies it's obviously murder. So I went out on the balcony and grabbed one of his legs just to make sure he didn't fucking drop! And that little scare sort of did it for Dave.

And any one of those clubbers that bought fish-tank-cleaning tablets thinking they were Es didn't get a very good buzz out of them but they had the cleanest piss in London.

A mate of mine, Boris, was in prison and when he came out he wanted to get back a gun that he'd plotted up in someone's house, under the immersion heater in the airing cupboard. Only trouble was that by the time Boris got out, the geezer in the house had moved. Boris, being Boris, decided to break in and have the floor-boards up in the middle of the night. The new house-owner heard him but he didn't come out; he rang the police from the bedroom phone. So Boris got caught but they nicked him for trying to steal the boiler! They thought he was a complete idiot. Which is better than getting nicked with the piece. He did eventually get that gun back, though. And for good measure he ripped out the boiler, put it in the double bed and tucked it in. Fucking hell, the difference between America and Britain – they leave behind cut-off horses' heads in people's beds; we leave behind heating systems! Mind you, that weren't the first boiler old Boris had bedded.

Steve McFadden, who plays Phil in *EastEnders*, rang me up one time and said they needed someone to play the part of a debt collector in one scene and rough up Phil. He said it was difficult for him to play the scene because the actors they usually chose he knew he could batter the living daylights out of in real life. So he asked me if I'd go up there for the role and throw him against the wall for a bit of reality! I would've really loved to appear in *EastEnders* but I was on my way to the fucking airport to go to Gibraltar with Joe just when he rang. There was no way out of it. Worse than that, when we got to Gibraltar the customs and undercover people were waiting and were all over us. Then the guy we'd gone to meet couldn't turn up so we ended up sitting in this casino for hours. When I saw the *EastEnders* scene on telly I was sick: they didn't look like they could threaten a fart out of a kitten. Afterwards Steve said, 'And I had to put up with having *that* done to me by *them*!'

My mate Brendan is a top silly cunt, and I mean that as a compliment. He's very, very funny is Brendan, especially when he's off his head, which is every weekend. He's a proper filth merchant as well; he'll shag anything with a pulse, and actually the pulse is optional. Why did Brendan cross the road? 'Cos his dick was in the chicken.

In Ministry of Sound one night we watched him cracking on to this bird that he thought was eyeing him up. He was stood there giving it with all the looks and smiles like he's last of the red-hot lovers, but we knew something he didn't. Anyway, after about ten minutes he plucks up the bollocks to approach her and found that she'd had her back to him all along. She had long black hair and he'd just imagined her face there! (Worse thing was, he said he'd only imagined her to be average-looking.) The friends of this girl were just cracking up.

Brendan had to go court this one time with his dad over some very underhand behaviour once again by our boys in blue. There was this bloke Frank in the next court who really thought he was something, but he weren't. He'd been given a ticket by a traffic warden, ripped it up, and then run him over. We all joke about traffic wardens but running the geezer over like that is just proper out-of-control, dickhead behaviour. So, this fella thinks he's jack-the-lad.

And this arsehole caused Brendan some proper grief in the court. He said some bad things in the waiting room which could've caused Brendan problems. Anyway, he saw Bren outside the courtroom and had words with him.

I was already down there with Phil, Mark Wicks and Tucker. I looked through the door window into the courtroom and this guy was in the dock giving evidence, and it didn't look like he was doing too well so I thought we'd go in and give him a hand.

Phil followed us in afterwards. Now Phil is really funny. He came into the court like a loud drunk, tripped up and fell, jumped up and went, 'SORRY!' You can imagine that in the perfect quiet of a court-room. It was fucking funny.

So we sat at the front and I put my arm around Brendan. The geezer in the dock tried hard not to look at us and just fumbled on. The jury looked at him looking at us and thought we were his mates. Which helped him out no end! Afterwards, he sent a message to Brendan saying, 'You and that bald cunt are dead.' You can imagine how shocked I was — I didn't even know I was bald!

Brendan turned to the fella that had brought the message and said, 'Will you go back and tell Frank that this is Dave's phone number so he can ring for a chat. The "bald cunt" is Dave Courtney, and that's his number if he'd like to make an appointment to see the Complaints Department.'

How we laughed.

Another time me and Brendan had to go see this geezer who was on the run. He was doing it all wrong — he'd left his missus and was going out with a 19-year-old barmaid; he was 46. He'd also bought a red Lotus sports car. We had to go meet him up at this little country pub in West Wickham. After we'd got there and had a drink me and Brendan went outside for a smoke of puff 'cos it wasn't allowed inside. I asked this fella if I could have the keys to the Lotus so we could skin up inside.

There was this cat on the bonnet, sat on the warm spot like they do. I picked it up, took it inside the car with us. When we were skinning up, the cat flipped up the lid of this big storage compartment that there was between the front seats, and then it got in and curled up inside. The lazy bastard was asleep in seconds. When we got out I closed the lid on it, I thought it'd make a funny suprise.

Anyway, we went back in to have a drink. Everyone started talking about how the pub was supposed to be haunted, people had been killed there, dogs wouldn't go in the cellar, and there was certain rooms people wouldn't sleep in. That kinda crap. A lot of people got the shits talking about it though. By the time we came out it was about two in the morning and I'd completely forgot about this fucking cat in the car.

As soon as I saw the car I remembered and I thought, Oh, this is gonna be funny. But the bloke and his bird got in the car, slammed the doors and nothing happened. Then he started it up and still fuck-all happened. So he pulled out of the car park and me and Brendan followed him waiting for something to happen. But then he floored it and the Lotus blasted off up the road into the dark.

Not a lot we could do then so we fucked off home. I did ring up to find out if anything had happened and the fella's brother answered and it was him that told me. Apparently, they'd driven off with this stupid mutt still asleep in the centre console box. When it woke up it started screaming, and you know how fucking freaky that cat-screaming sound is, don't you. Y'know, when you hear it at night it is very spooky. So, the geezer and his bird immediately start really freaking out, thinking the car's possessed by a fucking ghost. Then the cat sprang out into the car, spitting and hissing. The cat screamed, she screamed, he screamed. The woman opened the car door to get out — she was that petrified — but the seatbelt held her. The bloke said he'd instinctively turned his face away.

The cat shot out through the open door, though they didn't see it, and the Lotus flew straight up a bank and went slap-bang into a tree! She broke a collarbone and him both his feet. Fucking hell. Ooops. Not that funny a joke then, really.

Both of them are still in counselling 'cos they really thought it was a ghost. I did admit it, but I don't think they wanted to believe they'd written off a car, broke some bones and ruined two pairs of undies because of a bloody cat. It weren't really a ghost in the machine, more like a tiger in the tank.

Fuck knows what happened to the cat, but after jumping out of the car that must have been one sore pussy.

When we were making *Hell to Pay* I had the kind of problems that no director can ever have had, 'cos you'd only get these problems using real people, like I was doing. Not all of the geezers in the film actually got on with each other in real life but for the sake of the film they tried to put their differences aside.

So, we've got down to this big gun battle scene at the finale and I was explaining who gets shot by who . . . and this one geezer went, 'Hold it, Dave. Hold it.' I walked up to him and went, 'Yeah?' He said, 'That cunt ain't shooting me!' I said, 'He has to – you've just killed eight people!' He said, 'No. He ain't fucking shooting me.' In the end he said he'd let him do it if he was shot in the back. Five times.

Fuck me. So I went back over to the other bloke – at the same time thinking I'll bet Steven Spielberg never gets this shit – and told the other geezer. He went, 'Oh, no. What . . . in the back? What am I, a *cunt!*? No way.' Proper headaches I was having over them just *pretending* to have a row. They nearly had a row about how they should have a fucking row!

It ended up with them both wanting to draw at the same time and shoot each other in the head. And then their ghosts come back and have it out as well.

So anyway, where was I? Oh yeah, after I was hit by the machete . . .

8 THOUGHTS OF CHAIRMAN DAVE

- 'NEVER TRY TO DO A 24-CARAT WALK WITH 9-CARAT FEET.'

- 'IF YOU RISK NOTHING YOU LOSE NOTHING . . . BUT YOU GAIN NOTHING.'

- 'IF THE CAP FITS – NICK IT!'

- 'LET HE WHO IS WITHOUT SIN GET OUT MORE.'

- 'ONLY CARRY THE TOOL YOU'RE PREPARED TO DO THE TIME FOR.'

- 'CONTROL YOUR TEMPER, WALK AWAY, CALM DOWN – THEN GO BACK AT MIDNIGHT WITH A HOOD ON AND EIGHT MATES!'

- 'BEHAVE IN PRIVATE AS YOU WOULD IN PUBLIC.'

- 'LUCK IS FOR THOSE WHO DON'T PLAN AHEAD.'

- 'NEVER LOOK A GIFT HORSE IN THE ARSE – WRONG END.'

- 'HONOUR YOUR FATHER; FEAR YOUR MUM!'

- 'IF YOU CAN WALK THE WALK THEN YOU'RE ENTITLED TO TALK THE TALK.'

- ⊕ 'A WINNER NEVER QUITS AND QUITTERS NEVER WIN.'
- ⊕ 'TAKE NO SHIT AND TAKE NO PRISONERS.'
- ⊕ 'YOU'RE NEVER TOO OLD TO LEARN.'
- ⊕ 'MORE PEOPLE ARE KILLED BY TONGUES THAN GUNS.'
- ⊕ 'IT'S NICE TO BE IMPORTANT, AND IMPORTANT TO BE NICE.'

9 GUN NATION

In *Stop the Ride* there's a story about one time in Amsterdam when I had to make a run for it from a nuthouse out in the country. I know I was very lucky when the Dutch geezer made a bad call and went for my partner Dougie first. Which was an even worse call for Dougie. But it gave me the opportunity to at least attempt a shot at him before I got the next bullet. Not being the best shot in the world I was very pleased with the final result that day.

In that situation again I'd do the same thing but quicker. I think I was meant to die that day. That's how it felt. But I won the day. A bit of luck and a lot of good judgement saved me. Thank fuck though for the bit of luck, 'cos that you can't buy.

That was without doubt the most frightening gun battle experience I'd been in in my life. I'd been in gun battles before. Once on a farm by an old sewage works. The four of us: me, Terry Turbo, Dave Legano and Digger had a gunbattle which must have gone on for three, four minutes — which is a very long time in that situation — and only ended when everyone was out of ammo! We saw them running off which enabled us to run off the other way. (And when you're in a situation where you've got to run for your car, don't it always seem that you parked it a long way away! Take my word for it.)

One time I was in Spain doing a bit of business and whathaveyou, and a gun battle broke out. It was over a million quid that was to be brought back home, but a quarter of it was moody notes. It was all different foreign currencies which made it hard to know what was what. Which we didn't at first and took it away and counted it, and rumbled the forged gear. The guy that gave us the money-counting machine spotted the currencies which were fake.

They denied they done it, of course, and all hell broke loose, so I had to go back. It ended up with a full-blown gun battle in a place in the mountains, normally a very, very quiet scenic spot, but it was far from quiet that day. And they say Brits have a bad reputation on holiday! Fuck knows why. We were ever so polite. We even tried to *shoot* in Spanish.

Anyway, this place where we'd arranged for the meet was like an overnight stopover venue for trucks. There was loads of them parked up. Us four Londoners and the two Spaniards that were helping us and that had given us the guns, just ended up hanging about. I remember that the guns we were given were some Czecho-slovakian ones that I'd never heard of. I remember thinking, I hope this gun's easier to shoot than it is to pronounce or I'm fucked.

It went boss-eyed for a number of reasons. Firstly, they turned up firm-handed, and for another, it was dark. We were all pretty jumpy anyway. Not the best conditions. Then everything went totally pear-shaped pretty fucking sharpish when a gun was spotted on someone who wasn't supposed to be there. Everyone bolted then, ducking and diving for cover. It was weird 'cos it was as if someone had jumped up, blown a whistle and shouted, 'OK! Everyone start firing NOW!' 'cos it all kicked off at once and everyone started firing simultaneously. It was like synchronised shooting. And anyone and everyone who was carrying was firing all over the shop. There was loads of *pinging* and richocetting off the trucks.

It just goes to show how difficult it is to hit someone 'cos I bet thirty or forty bullets went off and no one got hit — and we were all fucking trying!

When it did kick off, this piece I had was, thankfully, easier to use than pronounce. But the whole event ended as quickly as it had started.

All you could really see was the flashes from the guns. The noise was amplified by the dark and by being up in the mountains. The truckers didn't stay asleep very long through that racket and they all woke up shitting themselves and got on their CB radios calling out 'Breaker! Breaker! Rubber duck!' and all that CB-talk crap.

They obviously called the Old Bill 'cos soon enough cop cars were screaming all over the fucking place.

Me and this other geezer had jumped into a skip lorry and hid in the back, so we just waited it out and when it got light we got out. All the lorries were starting up and our car, this Mazda, was still there because the police never knew it was one of ours. In the commotion we'd locked the keys in the car though, so we caved the back window in.

Someone saw us do that and called the Old Bill again! But we were long gone by that time.

We heard about it later and got told details from people that lived close by, and I can understand how they exaggerated on how many people were in the battle because I was there and it still seemed like there was 500 people shooting at us. That wasn't the case, obviously, but the way everyone was loosing rounds off it felt like 500. I can't lie and say it wasn't a fucking big buzz, 'cos it was, but it was also horrible, just shooting into the dark and hoping you'd got someone. That isn't the way to make you feel good.

I'll tell you what though, the films make it look really easy to shoot accurately enough to hit someone, but it ain't. It's not that easy at all. If someone's stood 50 feet away there's an awful lot of room for error; it only takes the barrel to be out by one degree and you've just successfully killed a wall or a potted plant. But odds on the geezer's still stood there trying to shoot you, and probably doing as badly.

That was the truth about the Wild West — it weren't quick-draws McGraws that won the day, it was Steady Eddies: it was the fucker with the nerve and experience to stand still and, while the other guy was blasting away, take careful aim and *bang*. Knowing how difficult it is in real life to actually hit a target don't half make you salute people who are good shots. It is a talent. In the Second World War top snipers were highly prized, and a cracking sniper could pin down and hold back a whole regiment of men for days on end. Just like in boxing — the perfectly timed peach is worth any flurry of punches.

Once you've lived through one of them kind of incidents then having a tear-up down the boozer with some geezer don't really faze you any more. Living through the worst thing makes you better for it. 'That which does not kill us makes us stronger' and all that. Bang on. Like if you got nicked for something that would give me five years it wouldn't feel so bad 'cos I've laid there under threat of a twenty.

First time anything happens, you're probably too shocked or scared to do or say the right thing. It gets easier. Like when that geezer pointed a gun at me in the foyer of a club; it wasn't bravery that made me turn my back on him, it was 'cos I was able to take the time to think properly. Doing that almost certainly saved me because he wasn't mad enough to shoot me in the back. So I could walk away.

Another one was at the Elephant & Castle when I was sitting in the back of this car and we went around and pulled up beside another one. The driver went like that, and shot the passenger in the other car in the face. Then it all kicked off.

Guns always come out in force during times of upheaval and change. Like when the rave scene first began it *was* all peace and love on the dancefloor but far from being lovey-dovey off the floor. There was some very naughty goings-on at the start while people were claiming territories after they realised what financial gain there was from this new drugs scene. Everybody realised it at the same time as well, so some pretty heavy artillery came out by people smelling a lot of money. People were getting very wealthy almost overnight. It caused the kind of old-fashioned territory wars that hadn't really been seen since the sixties.

It weren't so much the north/south London divided by the Thames any more 'cos raving disbanded all that by the fact that the youth just travelled to where the best club was, it didn't really matter which side of the river it was; from the Ministry in south London to the Gas in the West End or clubs north in Camden. But the wars started with the drug dealers and that's when the guns came out to play.

One night, while I was in a club preparing for a situation that was waiting for me outside, the DJ, MC Creed, stumbled across me getting ready — firearm-wise — for what I thought was gonna be this do-or-die situation outside the club. I don't think he's been able to look at me the same since that night. And every time he says hello to me he always gives me a severe cuddle to check I ain't got any unusual bulges. What actually happened that particular night I can't really go into too much; but put it this way, I wouldn't have lost that war . . . (You can read the full SP on club wars in *Raving Lunacy*.)

I've been shot at outside numerous clubs and pubs. Me and Big Marcus were shot at; Steve Bogart and me were fired at down in Bermondsey and three times at Tatchell Castle, the Queens and down in Dover. Fucking hell, that was a weekend and a half! And me and Ian Tucker got shot at a couple of times, and then there was that incident with Seymour in Tenerife only last year. I'm a *fucking* good dodger, let me tell you!

Every boy is always fascinated by guns from an early age and this fascination stays with you all your life. Loads of boys are into that but very few grow up to get the real things, like I did. I've seen, sold and slung some lovely guns. My favourites are the .44 Magnum Colts, Smith & Wesson, Uzis, M16s, Spats (the South African police riot gun) and, of course, the sawn-off.

There's something very British about a sawn-off shotgun, ain't there? That's one of the reasons I like it. Fucking awful to look down one though. You'd much rather be shot by one little bit of hot metal that might go through you than look up and see those two big black holes of a shotgun staring at you. That's fucking scary. Like looking into the eyes of a shark. No fucking mercy there. And a shotgun looks exactly like it will do *exactly* what it *will* do to you – cut you in half and throw the top bit of you over the fucking sofa into a soggy heap. A sawn-off even more so 'cos the spread is something terrible.

I had a fucking beautiful side-by-side sawn-off shotgun. I had it all chromed and then gold-plated by my mate Les. The handle was red rosewood. It was almost too pretty for something so powerful. It looked like an old-fashioned blunderbuss from a pirate ship.

The original *Lock, Stock and Two Smoking Barrels* story was taken from when I bought two guns over the telephone from a thief that had stolen them from a farm in Windsor. It was through a friend of my pals Wolfie, Dickie and Bish. I used to get a load of knocked-off gear from the gypsies down at the Queen Mother Reservoir Club.

I was getting firearms in abundance down there; and the two guns I bought over the phone I had sent down to a friend of mine that used to do all my gun alterations.

So the two shotguns I'd bought by phone got sent straight down to my mate and he sawed them off. When they got sent back up to me I saw that the guns were both Purdeys, which are like the Rolls-Royces of the gun world. I'm not saying they were in the best condition or that they were worth hundreds of grand each, but both together they were most probably worth a hundred large – definitely both together worth a hundred grand. And I had, in one fell swoop, made them worth about . . . three hundred quid! Bit of an antique specialist obviously, aren't I? Fucking hell, was I happy that day or what.

I kept the other two bits of the sawn-offs for years and years. I couldn't bear to ditch them 'cos I knew what they'd been worth. In fact, someone got nicked with the barrels that had been sawn off. The police did him by saying that he'd half-concealed the barrels in a blanket to make them look like they were whole guns (they did still have the sights on the barrel ends). Anyway, he got away with it.

So I kept my two bits of the guns until that geezer got nicked with the barrels and then I decided it was too risky to keep them. It's too easy for the Old Bill to pick and choose which bits of evidence to put up against someone. If they search someone's house they could lay out on a blanket a balaclava, a pair of gloves, an A–Z and a shotgun and then put that up before a judge and it looks very menacing.

Another man called Johnny McGee took a speedboat from outside my house which I'd sold to him and, strangely enough, there was a shotgun dumped in it. I'd been wondering where that had got to. Anyway, he'd already driven half way home when some tarpaulin came loose and Johnny had to stop and start clambering all over the boat to fix it. That's when he came across the shooter. He didn't know whether to dump it, save it, hide it or call me. When I did eventually get that shotgun back it had loads and loads of little snails living down the barrels.

My son Beau is a naturally good shot. Action Man from Doncaster is a good shot. And Big Marcus is a marksman. I'm not too bad at clay-pigeon shooting, but even in that I prefer a sawn-off. I just shot the throwing machine! When I went to Cannes to promote *Hell to Pay* I ended up on Mr *Playboy* magazine, Hugh Hefner's, yacht. Part of the party was shooting clay pigeons off the back of the boat. How fucking horny is *that*! Shooting guns off a yacht in Cannes surrounded by Playboy models. My dick was on a hair trigger!

Having a gun on you is like having the secret winner in your pocket, and the knowledge of that does give people an awfully big power syndrome. You can understand how some of these silly bastards on the news get into situations – some silly cunt in a tracksuit barricaded into a council house holding an Argos catalogue hostage! He's surrounded by 90 per cent of the local force backed up by an armed Tactical Response Unit and a helicopter, but that heavy bit of metal in his hand makes him half think he can take them on. 'Cos once you're holding that thing you can really fancy your chances. One of the worse side-effects of firearms – the warning they don't put on the tin – is that they can enlarge the balls and shrink the brain. Bad fucking combination.

The younger ones that carry them who are a bit more into the ego trip are walking around almost wanting someone to give them a chance to show it. Which can go against you 'cos once people know you carry a gun they don't want to fight you, they'll just shoot you. If you let them know you carry, you're showing your hand; and it leaves no room for manoeuvre and every excuse for them to escalate it. So the advantage is gone.

But if you have to, the smart money's always gonna be on using a revolver, not an automatic. Why ever use an automatic 'cos an automatic can jam. Sometimes they just do it automatically! These hip-hop street dealers run around with massive chrome auto .45s bigger than their heads but it's only got to jam once. And they do. I know a few people who have got fucked up big-time when they've had one jam on them. Like the Yugoslavian geezer I knew (see p. 111) whose gun jammed when he tried to shoot a couple of coppers. He got nicked and got life.

There ain't ever a time when you could afford to have your gun jam, is there, 'cos you wouldn't have the piece out in the first place unless it was fucking serious. They also leave shell casings as evidence. There's only one person who really favours a gun that might jam and that's whoever's about to get shot. At least it's an outside chance.

Getting hold of a piece is very easy to do now. Because of the hole they've made with the Channel Tunnel they're actually coming over here by the weight, not the item; and from the Eastern Bloc we are getting some very specialised weaponry.

The prices did actually go sky-high when they brought in the small firearms ban a few years ago but because of the quantity coming over here they are actually going back down in price. It is a booming market and there's many more people coming into the country from parts of Europe where guns are more easily found. These people are coming over here better equipped and more relaxed and less fearful around firearms. They've just come from a country where it was atural to have one stuck down your belt and shoot a few in the air very street party or voting day.

he price these days is between about £600 and £800 for a really ood one — meaning a revolver or automatic, maybe even with a ilencer if you're lucky. You can get an awful lot of second-hand nes cheaper but there's no point getting one when new ones are so heap. A second-hand one comes with an unknown history as well: might have already been used to do fuck-knows-what by fuck-nows-who.

he authorities have got so paranoid about firearms after the unblane killings that they tightened up on the wrong bits. They ade big changes to the wrong people, as they usually do. People ot hurt that shouldn't do like gun shops, sportsmen, armourers nd antique dealers, but it had no effect on where bank robbers ould get their guns and ammunition at all. The new law had fuck-ll effect whatsoever on the criminal world 'cos they'd always got eir guns illegally anyway. I mean ain't that obvious?! You know, ke some firm that are gonna do a bank, or some dealers that are lanning on taking out a rival gang will suddenly go, 'Oh, we better ot do that 'cos it's illegal to own a firearm.' It's like putting speed ameras at the Monaco Grand Prix! I don't think for one second ichael Schumacher would give a flying fuck.

I know a fella who is a dealer in deactivated firearms; he supplie film sets and it's where I got some of my stuff for the film. What th police have done to him though is outrageous — searched hi house, confiscated and took things, stole money from him. So he taking them to court. They've already cost him thousands.

It's another case of the authorities jumping on the wrong peopl with all their might just 'cos it looks good for the media. But th people they've stopped having guns ain't the sort of people they'v got to worry about having guns! Common sense. They've turne ordinary people into police-haters.

You don't need to be told by me what firearms and weaponry yo can get in this country 'cos if you just read the papers on any give morning, you'll see. Only last month they raided a place in Esse and found M16s, bazookas, limpet mines and a Stinger missile. geezers are getting that kind of advanced technical gear you ca rest assured they've Uzis, Magnums and shotguns tucked away a well. If you can get a fucking Stinger missile I'm sure you can get sawn-off!

Big Ron, who I knew, lived in Essex with his missus and had bee having a problem with certain people from another nightclub dow there where a couple of people had been killed on the door. Som people seemed to think Ron had something to do with it and he wa living with the threat of reprisals. Whether what happened next was connected or not nobody knows yet, but he was murdered one morning when he came out his house and someone pulled up on a pizza delivery moped, of all things, and put three rounds into him. He was a big geezer as well, was Ron, eighteen, nineteen stone. Big, big man. And he was done on his doorstep. He was also a wrestler, his nickname was 'Mayhem'.

That was one of loads of shootings and gun incidents that happened in that area over a few months. Things do seem to be getting worse on that score, particularly in certain notorious areas around Britain. In south London, where I live, there have been something like nearly 50 firearms incidents in the last three months! I'm gonna have to move soon, the fucking neighbourhood's gone right downhill. It's criminal.

A mate of mine had some family involved in one of the shootings. His sister was going out with this geezer who was on crack cocaine, which is an evil fucking thing, and he used to beat her up. Even in a pub in front of her family. So her dad told him to stop it, but the boyfriend told the old guy to go fuck himself. Now, the dad is an old fella who is also very ill from arthritis and he knows he can't protect his daughter from this bloke who is beating her up. Later on that night, at about half one in the morning actually, the boyfriend turned up at the dad's flat and started kicking off again. The old fella went into the bathroom, came back out with a gun, further arguments followed and he shot the cunt dead.

Now that old fella is really no more a murderer than I am a black ginger nun. Even though 'murderer' is what he now is. But if you've got the thing there, if you've got the piece too close to hand . . that's what it can lead to. If it hadn't been there and so easily got it never would have happened.

People do hide their guns in all sorts of different places. The catch-22 of the situation is that if you ever got caught with one indoors everyone would say 'What a fucking muppet, having it in there!' so you bury it somewhere. Trouble is, very, very rarely does someone jump out to have a go at you down the bottom of the garden, next to the paving stone by the shed where you hid your thing! You can hardly tell some geezer trying to kick your door in to hang on a minute while you get the plastic bag out from the bottom of the garden pond.

It is handy to have one plotted up somewhere but if you're high enough up in the world and smart enough to know, then you'll either be the sort of man who (a) would have a piece, but not tell anyone, and sort out his own problems, however serious ('cos you can't really trust anyone else with the knowledge of something that might get you life), or (b) someone with a very big Filofax, in which case you don't need no gun 'cos you have people who have them and they are at your disposal. You've got to work out which one of those two men you consider the most frightening.

I know that people who don't have anything to do with guns would find it completely unbelievable that they actually go off accidentally sometimes, but they do. You can even drop one and have it go off, and a lot of people don't always leave them in a safe place or put the safety on when they're out on a bit of work. It's not unheard of for people to shoot themselves in the foot, literally.

I do firmly believe in gun control. Without control you get your shots going everywhere! (And you might only get the fucker in the leg.)

Actually I do think guns should only be in the hands of people who know how to use them. Like armed robbers. I mean, you wouldn't want a paranoid epileptic with a stutter and a nervous twitch getting hold of a shooter, would you? Which in America he would do. Then he'd join the police.

How the fuck did the LAPD get away with that beating-up of Rodney King all those years ago; when they were all caught on video, remember? Well, I know they didn't get away with it 'cos they got filmed – camcorder nation! – but they never got charged. Yet another case of a suspect recklessly throwing his head against a policeman's boot – twenty-nine times. It's so easily done. Mind you, Los Angeles did then blow up into massive riots because the cops got off, so that was the payback.

In America they shoot each other, in Britain we bore each other to death talking about the weather. American suicides shoot themselves in the head; British suicides kill themselves slowly with daytime telly. Richard and Judy must be the king and queen of manslaughter.

Did you know, by the way, that you can actually shoot yourself two or three times in the head? Like once isn't enough. Some deaths that are first put down as murders later turn out to be suicides. Because – and get this – after the first shot has killed you, the trigger finger can suffer something called 'cadaveric spasm' and carries on squeezing out bullets. Fucking hell. Bad luck if you change your mind after the first shot. And a proper baffler for the local plod too, I would imagine.

Here's another puzzler for you: if someone shoots someone that's already dead ... what are they guilty of? (Apart from wasting a bullet.) Well, actually, it's murder, in the eyes of the law anyway. I met this geezer in court once who was up for just that charge. He'd been at the scene of a murder and the dead geezer was, without a shadow of a doubt, *dead* – brains-on-the-wall-type dead, with witnesses to prove it. This other bloke then, for whatever reason, put a bullet in the body as well. Later he was caught and charged with murder along with the geezer who'd actually killed the bloke.

How does that make sense? How can you kill a dead body? Even the autopsy said the first shot killed him. So the worse thing the second geezer could be guilty of is something stupid like 'grievous bodily body shooting' or 'abuse of a corpse'. Or maybe bad timing. But never murder. Like if you shagged a bird after she was already pregnant, that don't make you daddy.

I'm glad guns aren't massively available over here 'cos we'd end up like the States where all the schoolkids are shooting each other, or every road rage incident is a full-blown war. In America you can't even throw a snowball at a nun without her pulling a Magnum from under her habit and blowing your fucking head off.

Praise God and pass the ammunition.

10 WEAPON OF CHOICE

What someone picks up off the table before they leave the house can decide the rest of their life. And that's without even using it. You'd be looking at a maximum penalty of ten years for just being caught carrying a gun. If you're caught with it loaded it's ten years, set. It don't really cut much ice the fact that you haven't used it! It don't work like that. You don't get medals for *restraint*. Fact is, if someone's got it in the car they're definitely not on their way to a prayer meeting (unless the vicar's properly fucked somebody off) and they're probably not that far away from either using it or handing it over to someone. And if they can prove that you were on your way to do something then they start bumping the sentences up. All that for just having it in your pocket, or your car, or a hollowed-out Bible!

Only a proper wild card would constantly carry a gun around for no good reason other than the carrying of it. But I've met a few of those in my time.

A very good friend of mine from the former Yugoslavia used to carry a shooter constantly. He was down at Margate one day when he got stopped by the Old Bill on a spot search. He was buzzing at the time. When they tried to search him he pulled out the gun and tried to shoot the copper. It went click-click-click, jamming, so he dropped it and it fucking went off when it hit the floor! So he picked it up, tried to fire it but it jammed again: he dropped it a second time and it went off again. The coppers finally realised the score, chased the geezer and beat the living fuck out of him with their nightsticks. He got life. He's now in Broadmoor, regretting the day he chose an automatic.

I've said it before, only use the tool you are prepared to do the time for. I'm not prepared to walk around carrying something that every time I use it I risk getting life because of the possibility of killing someone. I'm sure the thing that got Kenny Noye life was what tool he decided to put in his pocket before he went out that morning, because when he got into a road-rage fight with this six foot one karate kid who was twenty years younger than Noye and six inches taller, survival instinct was always gonna make him go for the tool. He did, and both of them paid the price.

Best thing is if you're handy with your fists, because unless you're a boxer you can't exactly be classed as carrying a weapon. Although even giving someone a slap has led to people crying murder. That happened to Lenny McLean. He was in the Hippodrome once when this bloke ran riot naked on the dancefloor. Lenny ended up collaring him and giving him a backhander. The geezer left the club, went barmy in the streets, got arrested and died later that night.

Next day Lenny was charged with his murder. He called on my old brief Ralph Haeems.

It ended eventually with a trial at the Bailey where it came out that the guy who'd died should have been on medication; and one of the medical experts said his death could've even been caused by the coppers using a stranglehold restraint when they'd nicked him. Lenny was found not guilty.

On the track that I did with Tricky on the album *Product of the Environment* I say, 'If you carry a gun and something happens/you're more likely to pull out the gun and use it/If you carry a knife when you're losing a fight/you'd pull it out and stab him/If you carry a duster you'd pull it out and break their jaw and knock them out . . .'

Now, breaking someone's jaw is gonna win you the fight but it won't get you buried alive in a jail if they nick you for it. I'd do whatever bit of bird that got me. Whereas plunging someone or shooting them will bury you as well as them.

A doorman mate of mine, Jo-Jo, went one better when he lost his hand in a car crash. It was crushed to bits. It had to come off so he had a fucking big pirate's hook fitted! It looked mental. He could walk around with that on the end of his arm and not get nicked.

Anyone else would've got done for carrying. Bloody good arse-scratcher as well.

I've got a proper little selection of knuckledusters at home now. Brass ones, gold ones, aluminium lightweight ones, silver ones, and a gold and diamond studded one. That leaves a pretty little pattern behind on the jaw, I can tell you. It's worth over twenty odd grand though, so I don't take it out often. Only special occasions like chinning royalty.

The police come down on me for promoting them but when I worked on the doors, if twenty lairy geezers turned up on a stag do, or the club had people in there carrying knives and sprays or even guns, then I think I should've been fucking commended for standing there with just a duster! Thank you, officer!

Anyway, I only ever carry them now as a prop for Jen's stage show. Your honour . . .

The history of the knuckleduster is that they've been around in some form for fucking ages, right back to big spikey ones used by gladiators. But the modern invention came from the American Civil War. The cavalry used to drive along carrying their swords and by the time they came to battle they were fucked, so they made a more manageable grip on the sword handle, hence the shape of the duster. Then they found that when they were in battle the sword blade might get snapped off, and when it did it left quite a handy little tool behind, and one favoured as a weapon in itself.

Personally I believe it was as important an invention as fire, the wheel and electricity – at least in my house! That's what I think, anyway. The Pope may disagree with me; but then he's probably never had to try deck a geezer twice his size.

Knuckledusters are a weapon that as long as you can throw one punch *that* way – meaning forward – then you are odds-on favourite to win the fight, 'cos if you can throw a good shot anyway then once you've got the brass on that punch it will be worth ten: if they parry it it will break their wrist, if they block it it'll crack a bone, if you catch the chest it'll break a rib, or you could break a jaw; and if you get them in the belly it'll bend them over. A knuckleduster ain't gonna kill someone (unless they, and you, are very unlucky), but it will fucking hurt! I can handle three years in prison for assault – I wouldn't like to do fifteen years just 'cos I made a bad choice of tool and then got in a row with a geezer down the shops.

Another thing, make sure it's rounded at the edges 'cos you don't even want to split skin, you want to go *bang* and knock him out. If you've got anything sharp, where it meets the bone it'll split skin and that actually goes to GBH; but if you chin him with the brass and just knock him out it ain't as serious a charge. So rub the edges down, silly. It'll deliver the same punch, so fuck the blood spilling . . . you're not on colour telly! You don't get points for drama.

I have seen two guys fighting that had a duster each. I've seen two guys throw a punch at each other and one duster hits the other, hand to hand. It sounded like they were having a fucking sword-fight. I've seen one guy throw the first punch, miss, get off balance and drop his duster, and the other geezer picked it up and turned him into fucking mincemeat. So, little tip, make sure that it fits! How you do that is with a roll of plaster. Keep that roll of plaster to roll it around and make it snug on your hand. Or, if you're clever, wrap the whole thing in plaster so it doesn't really stand out and that way everyone will think you've done it with your hand, you tasty bastard! Or you can put it on first and then put an extra large pair of gloves on top and no one will notice . . .

Now who else on the bookshelves are you gonna get these tips from? Jeffery fucking Archer? Jamie Oliver? (Maybe from Delia Smith though, she looks like a tough old bird.)

I've been hit by a duster myself three times (not counting that time Jen threw a J-cloth at me). Once on the chin but luckily it weren't really that hard a shot to begin with, and I think I was turning my head at the time as well so it didn't have the effect. But it still *did* have an effect! They always do. Once I got hit on the back of the head, which made it feel like my fucking eyes were falling out; and once I got done on the shoulder blade and that put my shoulder out of sorts. And all those shots weren't even from proper fighters really, just half-weights that happened to have a good tool. Any one of those shots from a proper bloke would've put you in shit deep enough to put a lilo on.

Proper punchers don't flail their arms — you cock it like a gun until you see the target and fire it, *BOOM!*, and if you've got a duster on it's devastating. But if you're one of them who flails his arms about like an epileptic on the spin-dry cycle then the whack won't be hard enough to be a proper pain. It'll be a hurt not a pain. There is a difference.

The duster has enabled me to beat people that I cannot beat in the old, traditional one-to-one. I would have probably lost 50 per cent. But usually it's the huge geezers who are up for the one-to-ones anyway so I was just evening things up a bit! That's me, you see — a strong sense of fair play. Call me old-fashioned.

In relation to the knuckleduster, the law stands like this . . . about twenty feet away, legs crossed, looking very worried. No, it is actually, surprise surprise, an offensive weapon. Ooops. Or a 'Statutory instrument' as it's called in THE CRIMINAL JUSTICE ACT 1988 (OFFENSIVE WEAPONS) ORDER.

(a) a knuckleduster, that is, a band of metal or other hard material worn on one or more fingers, and designed to cause injury, and any weapon incorporating a knuckleduster;

There's some other interesting stuff in there:

(b) a swordstick, that is, a hollow walking-stick or cane containing a blade which may be used as a sword;
(c) a 'handclaw', being a band of metal from which a number of sharp spikes protrude, and worn around the hand;
(d) a 'footclaw', being a bar of metal from which a number of spikes protrude, and worn strapped to the foot;
(e) the weapon known as a 'belt buckle knife', being a buckle which conceals a hidden knife;
(f) the weapon known as a 'blowpipe' or 'blow gun', being a hollow tube out of which darts are shot by the use of the breath.

Fuck me! Is that a totally mental list or what! And where do the people who make these laws fucking live? – 'cos I don't want to move anywhere near there. A blowpipe? When was the last time you heard of one of them mentioned on the news: 'Reports are coming in of a man holed up in a council flat keeping police at bay with a blowpipe and poisoned darts. It is believed he snapped after he went to Blockbuster video and found they didn't have a copy of the film *Zulu*.'

And a '*footclaw*'?! What the fuck's that about? I've only ever seen one of those in that James Bond film. Hardly practical though, is it? You'd have to wear bleedin' sandals all day long. And for that you'd deserve to get attacked.

I'd love to see a villain in a film wearing that whole kit and kaboodle, (a) to (f). Rattling like a box of chisels, limping 'cos of the 'footclaw' and trying not to forget about the 'handclaw' in case he goes to pick his nose. Come to think of it though, that swordstick sounds half tasty. But not half as tasty as (a) of course.

In terms of punishment I think it's six months inside for first possession of a duster, a year for the next one, and then technically I suppose you could get life for the next one under the 'three strikes and you're out' rule. I don't think that there is, in the law's eyes, a remotely arguable excuse for carrying one. There could be a reason, however stupid it might sound, for having a pickaxe handle, an axe, a knife, a hammer, a bat or even a fucking gun. You can manipulate most of them. But a duster ain't made to do anything else. You can't exactly say it's for nothing other than punching someone in the fucking head. Unless you use it as a prop in your media career . . . like I do. /thank you.

Oh, wait a minute, tell a lie, I think I have just found a reason for carrying a duster other than the obvious one. Jen's found it on a website. Ain't the computer a blinding thing? We were just going through looking for the Teletubbies website — aren't they sexy little beasts? (or is that just me) — but we found loads of knuckleduster websites instead. Easy mistake to make. Touch. Anyway, there's this website called 'Mr Knuckles' which sells knuckledusters and there's also photos of all the different types.

The clever bit is, to get around the restriction on selling them as weapons they market them as paperweights! Or the duster with spikes on it is described as an icepick, and the one with a jagged edge is called a meat tenderiser! (That's one way of putting it . . .)

Funny that, but it must work as a way of getting around the problem of selling it as an offensive tool. It seems too obvious to work, though, y'know what I mean? 'Cos I'm sure if the Old Bill raided my house and found an Uzi on the coffee table (which they wouldn't of course). I'd have a fucking hard time convincing them it was a paperweight for holding down my council tax bills (anyway, that little job would need something much heavier, like an M16).

Anyway, so these brass and silver fuckers on the website with spikes and points and jagged edges and all that, they have got to be the most dangerous fucking paperweights I've ever seen. I bought twelve.

In fact, I was so impressed I bought the company!

By now I've turned the knuckleduster into my emblem. Instead of the original emblem choice of a nun being taken roughly from behind by an Alsatian. Difficult to get that one printed on T-shirts. I've got a duster tattooed on my chest, one is shaved in the back of my missus's haircut, and a gold one worn round her neck on stage; it's the emblem on our records, the prop most used in my photos and it's become a major sign in my life . . . and did you know if you lay out two back to back they look like a butterfly! That's one for the hippies out there. See, I have got a sentimental side.

It can be a force for good. Especially on someone's chin. Also during my 'Audience With . . .' tours I auction off one of my dusters for charity (no, really!) at each venue: in Sheffield someone bid £500, next night in Doncaster we got £300, and up in Sunderland someone spent £200. Not a bad little tally.

So all hail the duster. It doesn't even want to be a spy. It don't even wanna dress up and pretend to be anything else! It's proud to be a duster. It's held in very high regard in my house and is worshipped and prayed to every morning: 'Our Father, who art carrying a tasty tool . . .'

11 DODGY MEETS TRICKY

Tricky, you all know Tricky? Funny little geezer who wears dresses in his videos. Well, actually we'll forgive him that 'cos he *is* a bit of a musical genius and also an absolutely top fella as well. He's had a bit of naughtiness in his own past but now he's forging ahead in the music world. Good luck to him.

He decided he wanted to make an album with his music and the voices of well-known naughty geezers talking on it. Bloody good idea if you ask me. And he did ask me. So I said yes, thanks very much, see you in the studio.

Along with me there was Roy Shaw, Freddie Foreman, Joey Pyle, Charlie Richardson, Tony Lambrianou, Jack Adams, Tommy Wisbey, Bernie Lee, Frank Fraser, Tony Guest. We all had to sit down in Jack Adams' house and do our bit; talk about our lives and what we thought, etc. So . . . twelve hours later when I was still sat there gabbing away into the mic, they suggested we call it a day. I said they couldn't call it a day 'cos it'd only been twelve hours — that's only half a day! We still had another twelve to go.

Only a slight exaggeration there, but it was fun. And the album turned out to be the absolute bollocks. It's called *Product of the*

Environment and it's on the Palm Pictures label. Buy it and you'll have your own criminal record.

In Italy they did a two-hour documentary about the project in preparation for a conference that was being held in Milan. What it was was a conference on world media crime which was actually organised by the CIA, believe it or not. In order to choose who they wanted to speak they sent some film-makers over to Britain to make a documentary, like a showreel of different naughty people. Then from that film, me, Bruce Reynolds and Mark Munden, the director of *Bermondsey Boy* (the first documentary about me), were chosen to go over.

Since making the record Tricky and me have become pals and a very interesting geezer he is too. I even went over to New York for a weekend out with him and Quentin Tarantino.

I also did a little interview with Tricky for *Front* magazine. It turned out this way:

Tricky had always wanted to hear those tales, those frightening yet compelling stories from the mouths of the criminal under-world. And, amazingly, his keyboardist Gareth Bowen managed to track down the crème de la crème of the country's hardest criminal fraternity, and get them to agree to him recording their *accounts of life on the wrong side of the law. Tricky provided the musical landscape to plant these dark words in, and the resulting album – **Product of the Environment** – contains tales from the likes of bare-knuckle fighter Roy 'Pretty Boy' Shaw, 'Mad' Frankie Fraser, Charlie Richardson and, of course,* Front's *Dodgy Dave Courtney, who grabbed the opportunity for a swift natter with Tricky . . .*

You don't mind if I do a quick interview with you, do you?
What fucking option have I got? Tell them to put me down and let go of the stranglehold on my neck and I'll talk to ya. You only had to ask. Jesus, man!

What do you say to the people who think you're weird?
They're right . . .

Have you come into the firing line much by doing this album with me and all the chaps, and – if so – what's your defence?
It was a fantastic chance for all these legendary men – including yourself, of course – to say in public that crime ain't the way to go, that it ain't all glamorous, and that babies ain't born naughty and criminally minded. They become a product of their environment as they get older – that's all of you, Mr Freddy Foreman, Mr Roy Shaw and Mr Fraser, Mr Lambrianou, Mr Tommy Wisbey, Mr Jo Pyle, Mr Charlie Richardson, Bernie and, last but not least, Mr Dave

Courtney. That's why the album is called *Product of the Environment*, and that's the way you people are, like it or not.

Were we easy to work with?
Well, I wasn't in the studio with any of you! It was a very talented group of men led by Gareth who got you to talk. Besides, who's got the arsehole to tell any of you that you were shit? I certainly ain't! Luckily, you were all very, very good. In fact, you were all so individual, personal and truthful that it was very moving indeed.

Up till now, we thought the likelihood of being on *Top of the Pops* was nil – d'you reckon we've got any chance of ending up on the show?
Oh yes, definitely, definitely! At least three tracks will be put out as singles, and I just know they'll be big; very, very big! And before you ask, Dave, yes, yours is going to be one of those singles. In fact, it's the first one, I think . . .

How did that tune you and that little hard nut geezer out of *East Enders*, Steve McFadden, do? Pink Floyd's *The Wall*, wasn't it?
Fuckin' excellent, as it happens. Gareth has got Sony very interested, and now we're back in the studio doing a few more tracks. The only poxy thing is Steve can fucking sing, and he makes me sound a proper prick, like a football hooligan shouting from the stands! But that can be good – it's a good sound if it's done right.

When we said we'd do the record for Save the Children they said they didn't want the money. Why do you think that was?
Well, the way the government brainwashes the public into believing you're all evil men ... no doubt that's got something to do with it. But who are Save the Children to say no? Do they honestly think the child that gets some food will mind if the money for it was made by some men who were once in prison? Looking at it that way, you gotta ask yourself, who's the real criminal? People want to hear it from the men themselves, and 'Don't copy us' is a really good message for the youth to hear from men like your good selves.

Seeing as you and your band must be quite well off – all your albums hit platinum and your concerts sell out – why are you all so fucking scruffy?
You cheeky fucker! It's fashion, man! Laid back, comfy ... This shirt cost more than most people's suits! Scruffy? Ha!

So, what are the boxing gloves doing in your holdall? Expecting a bit of aggro, are we?
I train every day, bag work and running, and I often have my man hold these pads for twenty minutes or so. It's good for the heart and brain, and both of mine are pumping really good, thank you. Do you still train, Dave?

**No, every time I feel a little bit out of shape or unfit, I buy a
bigger knuckleduster . . .**
I've got to do my make-up now, Dodge. See you at the boxing do
tomorrow, Mr Stein's show at the International. Why you look at me
that way?

I never knew you wore make-up! So, you ARE weird . . .
It's for me performance, you silly fucker!

The words to my track on the *Product of the Environment* album
went something a little like this:

> I'm Dave Courtney,
> My position in sort of the London crime scene is
> I have under my command five hundred six foot flat-
>   nose geezers
> I'm looked at as an army
> I'm called in London the yellow pages for the
>   underworld
> It's not being a villain I find addictive:
> it's the lifestyle around it
> The class went out of crime when the only crime left
>   to do was drugs
> Most of my wealth has come through debt collecting
> I do specialised debt collecting

I go all around the world chasing people
for money that they owe everybody else
And if the price was right I would be prepared
to do anything to retrieve the debt
I would be prepared to go to any lengths to retrieve
Thirty per cent of two hundred grand,
apart from kill somebody
My choice of weapon is a knuckleduster
If you choose a gun then you've got to be prepared
to do fifteen years for murder
If you carry a gun and something happens
You're more likely to pull out the gun and use it
If you carry a knife, when you're losing a fight
you'll pull it out and stab him
If you carry a duster, you'd pull it out and break their
    jaw and knock him out
The good times are good, really good
but the bad times are really, really bad
They outweigh the good times
There's got to be an easier way to earn a living apart
    from dodging bullets and doing a load of bird
When I sit back and think of my life so far:
the bullet holes, the different prisons I've been
    banged up in;
the so-called glamour of the crime game . . .

it's all bollocks, really
It's so sad when you want to go see a friend
and you have to go up and down the country
I'm finished with it.
Four times I've been to prison on remand
I ain't going to prison no more
I'm finished with it.

Now does that sound like someone who's glamorising crime? I don't think so. You see, if people like the way I handle myself now and also like the things I do *after* my life of crime has ended, then that's a different ball game, ain't it? It's not the same thing as they're complaining about, and ain't it lucky I don't give a flying *fuck* anyway!? Touch!

12 ALWAYS SHAG A NATIVE

I love travelling. I can say 'not guilty' in ten different languages, even Scouse – 'Wha'? Me? *Meeer*der!?' I've even done a debt collection job as far afield as Australia. Thank fuck it was expenses paid: Down Under – very far away, big fucking country, lotsa fucking sheep. We came back with £200,000 and foot-and-mouth! This geezer had ripped someone off for so much dough he'd run off to Australia and bought his own beach-front bar. As if I couldn't find him from Peckham . . .! Silly bollocks.

After you've travelled that far and found someone, you don't really need to do the threatening bit. Just turning up does the job. We threw in a little 'promise' anyway, just for good measure, and a bit of a laugh. Something to do with him going swimming and local sharks I seem to remember. Awww . . . the good old days! I look through my passport sometimes at the different airport stamps and go all misty-eyed at the memory of dangling people off balconies in some of the world's most beautiful countries. Call me old-fashioned: I'm just a romantic old fool, aren't I? Old soppy bollocks.

Kids these days don't think they've been on holiday unless they fly. So take them to Blackpool and throw them out the fucking hotel window. I'm not cruel – make sure there's a pool below. Anyway, when I was a kid we'd go to this place called Cliftonville. It's between Ramsgate and Margate. It was always raining. They should've renamed it Floodgate. My mum took us there every year. There was a dolphinarium there and I thought it was the absolute bollocks. Fucking hell, seeing a real dolphin after only pictures was wicked. I'll let you in on a secret though, they're a lousy shag. Kept blowing water out the hole.

Which reminds me, when you do travel always make sure you try the local dishes. And between each shag, eat some of the local food as well. No, you can get a proper taste of a country from its women (and that's something you won't hear Judith fucking Chalmers saying on *Wish You Were Here*!). So always shag a native before you leave. You've got wild, sexy, curvy birds in Brazil; tiny, hot, naturally horny women in Thailand; loud and upfront ladies in America; and weightlifting, alcoholic gorillas with Aids in Russia. Actually I ain't ever been to Russia so that's just a wild guess. There are two Russian sisters that work as table dancers at a favourite haunt of mine in London, and they're both stunning. So there you go. And I bet you will.

So get to Brazil to check the beaches and women in Rio. I went there for Ronnie Biggs' seventieth birthday with Bruce and Nick Reynolds, Roy Shaw, Tony Hoare, loads of others and loads of press following us out there. There turned out to be over a hundred people at Ronnie's house for his party. I had a delivery from Charles Bronson, a hand-made birthday card he'd sent me to give to Ronnie. Inside Charles had written, 'Never walk backwards into a madman's cage – especially if you are wearing a kilt.' Well, it's the thought that counts!

Rio is a horny, horny place but also probably the most dangerous place I've been to. It's dangerous 'cos there's so much poverty and that makes men desperate. And desperate is very dangerous. It's worse for the men than the women 'cos the women can always trade in sex, but the men can't. And at £12 a night you might as well have a hundred quid's worth!

One of the best trips I ever had was to Phuket in Thailand. If you're pissed off with your life I highly recommend you just say, 'Phuket!' and fuck off to Thailand. I went with my Jen, no kids, and we had a very very sexy holiday. Thailand's like Brazil in that it's a very raw and sexy country, but because they're so open about it it ain't at all smutty. That don't come into it. I think in that respect they are leading the way.

I was out in Mombasa in Africa one year with some of the fellas looking for Tony's Lambrianou's black mamba, and we bumped into a geezer deep in the jungle and he said, 'Shirley Bassey says hello' and then ran off. Or so Tony tells me, time and time again.

In the middle of Mombasa the Americans have built a big casino. You just can't believe you're walking through the undergrowth and then *boom*, there it is, this building out of nowhere with people milling about in dinner suits. But still slap-bang in the middle of Africa. There is a dress code, though. You're not allowed in without a spear, and absolutely *no* members of the Chumba Wumba tribe. Fucking troublemakers. As the local doormen say, 'There's a plate in your lip so you're not coming in!'

Yeah, the Yanks still run it over there like it's in the middle of Las Vegas. You could tell they were on the naughty side 'cos even the wildlife were wary of them.

Dave's Travel Tips

1) Don't take anything it would upset you to lose. So no favourite knuckleduster.
2) Take a suitcase full of charity shop crap and pick up a better one off the carousel at the other end (although you might spend the rest of the holiday in a pensioner's frocks and support tights).
3) Get an American Express card. There's a million dodgy things you can do now they've guaranteed to give you your money back.
4) Don't forget your toothbrush. And a fuck-load of Durex.

5) Remember, we don't actually *own* half the world any more.
6) Foreign police are absolute cunts, just in another language.
7) And remember, sign language is universal, so as long as you have the use of two fingers you can still always say 'OK', 'Peace' and 'Fuck you'.
8) Keep all personal narcotics firmly up your arse when flying. It's safer. And nice!

And Don't Forget the Lingo, Gringo

Whichever country you're visiting make sure you learn a few phrases before you go. In general it's pretty useful to be able to say the following in the local lingo:

(1) 'No comment' (2) 'Get me a lawyer' (3) 'Not guilty' (4) 'How much does a bent copper cost then?' (5) 'No, of course I won't come in your mouth, officer' (6) 'I didn't mean that kind of "bent"!' (7) 'I'd like to thank the jury' (8) 'I always had faith in the justice system of . . . (*country's name*)' (9) 'Thanks' (10) 'No thanks' (11) 'Fuck off' (12) 'Hello, babe' (13) 'Do you take it up the arse?' (14) 'All back to mine then!' (15) 'Where's the Seven-eleven?'

And one that *I* find especially useful: 'No, I am *not* fucking Kojak! Anyway, he's dead!'

When you've mastered them you'd better brush up on a few useful bits of dialogue and phraseology in the lingo of whichever specific country you're fucking off to. Here they are in no particular order of childishness!:

SWEDEN

1) 'I would like to firebomb Ikea. Thank you.' 2) 'Are Volvos your big joke on the world?' 3) 'Explain fucking Abba to me.' 4) 'I've made a massive mistake coming here – where's the emergency exit?'

CHINA

1) 'Bruce Lee's a wanker.' 2) 'Yes, your dog's very nice, but I've already eaten, thanks.'

JAPAN

1) 'Look at me when I'm talking to you.' 2) 'Please stop bowing, you keep nutting me in the knackers.' 3) 'Why the fuck did kamikaze pilots wear crash helmets anyway?'

GERMANY

1) 'My nan says thanks for killing my grandad, he was a miserable bastard.' 2) 'Which silly fucker forgot to put a gate in the Berlin Wall?' 3) 'Don't mention the war.'

ARGENTINA
1) 'Shame about the Falklands but you did fuck us later in the World Cup with that fat little cunt Maradona.'

ISRAEL
1) 'Hitler, eh? What a cunt.' 2) '. . . OK, forget the bacon . . .'

SPAIN
1) 'If you just *shot* the bull it'd be over much quicker.' 2) 'Now how much for half a ton?' 3) 'You have such lovely sideburns, señorita!'

ITALY
1) 'I'm sorry, I didn't realise she was a nun.'

GREECE
1) 'Is that a kebab in your pocket or are you just pleased to see me?' 2) 'Could you please stop sucking your moustache, I'm trying to eat. Thank you, madam.'

RUSSIA
1) 'Fuck me it's cold!' 2) 'Where is the nearest lap-dancing club?' 3) 'Please don't fucking shoot me.'

COLOMBIA
1) '*How* much? OK, I'll have a ton and a half, please. Cheers.'

BIRMINGHAM, ENGLAND

1) 'Hello. We come in peace from big metal bird in sky!'

The one place I haven't been yet that I'd really like to visit is Cuba. For one thing I'd feel like I'd died and woken up in cigar heaven — 'Havana good time, wish you were here!' And another thing, I think that Fidel Castro is the absolute nuts. What a man. He took over the country when he was only 32 and freed the people from a police state. A-fucking-men to that. He's been prime minister ever since, over forty years, and he's now in his seventies. Top cigar smoker and a proper leader of men. The geezer just won't be bullied. Not many countries have defied America and won, or at least held their own. And you know it's still illegal to travel from America to Cuba! I do like those places in America where I've been but it's a bit rich how they call themselves the Land of the Free.

It's been proved since that in the sixties the CIA actually had a plan to try to assassinate Castro with a poison-dipped cigar. That sounds like one of those things that's so stupid it might have even worked if they'd got it together.

I don't know what Bill Clinton's excuse was for dipping his cigar but I'll bet it tasted better than Castro's.

Anyway, there really is no place like home. Especially my home because as you know, it's a big fucking white castle of a house in Plumstead!

I was sat in the car waiting at a zebra crossing the other day and across it were parading this group of people: the blokes in white baggy pants and smocks and turbans, and the women in full-length black gowns and veils with their eyes peeping out. I thought, honestly, I just *don't* know — the fucking Welsh are taking over, aren't they?

But of all the cities in the world none of them really does it for me like London. Even now Soho and Leicester Square at night still do it for me, even though I'm now 41 and should know better, probably. There's still a buzz there for me.

So buy me a penthouse pad over Stringfellows and I'll be happy.

13 ENGLAND'S DREAMING

The biggest criminal problem that this country will know, in my opinion, and what will be the biggest turning point in crime in Great Britain, will be when the Russians and other Eastern Europeans decide to show their hand. Maybe five years from now. But they *are* here.

They're not just hard nuts, they're trained killers. They're fucking sleeping assassins. They are not gonna show their hand until they've got all the aces, then they'll go *BOOM*.

They're coming in strong financially, first of all, and buying up London. Buying up hotels and mansions and nightclubs, but quietly. And there's ex-KGB people over here masquerading as Serbs and Croats and Christ knows what else, so we're not alarmed by this influx of one nationality.

Over here we'd go into a pub and punch a geezer. Over there they'd walk into a bar and shoot someone in the head. They use hand grenades, machine guns, rocket launchers. It's a completely different ball game. They know suffering from early on in their everyday lives, just ordinary people, and they grow as hard as fuck. So imagine how cold the naughty ones of the pack are. In fact 'naughty' don't even sum it up. We've got our own thing going on but the English villain will get fucking destroyed within minutes 'cos they'd be facing KGB-trained killers that have now decided to be gangsters. The USSR has broken up and all the guns, surveillance equipment, explosives, and people who know how to use them, are going spare. They also have the kind of patience and coldness that to us seems fucking insane (only the Orientals can compete with it – I know first hand from seeing a Triad execution in London).

For instance, they will stay here and work for four, five, six years so that they can come out of the woodwork when the time is right, or when they are called for. And Russian gangsters, like Chinese and Japanese ones, really do live up to the word. They're quiet, cold, unforgiving. They don't doorstep bodies; they don't have riots; they don't have wars. They will chop you up.

They will not allow you to perceive a large Russian community. It seems too much like a threat. There may well be an out-and-out plan to take over British crime. Russian gangs – living what they've lived, the way they've had to live, and what they *haven't* got – have looked over here, like someone looking into a mansion, and thought, Fucking hell, what riches they've got there! And what a bunch of wankers running it, in their view. That's how they view it – British gangsters and villains have no chance whatsoever of winning the inevitable confrontation with these people.

England has no idea. These people won't group up like the Chinese in Chinatown so you can count how many there are and what they're doing and who with. They don't want to go like the blacks have gone to Brixton: visible, easily pinned down and tracked and traced. They want to be invisible. It's cleverer to disperse.

I'm telling you through people I know who *know*; who said to me before that I'd never heard them say anything that wasn't right and this is what's going to happen. It was said to me long enough ago for me to be able to watch the beginnings and see it's only a matter of time. We may not even realise it's happened at all if they take the smart option of using Brits to front the operations once they take them over – which they will do.

These fuckers take over small nations. They assassinate presidents. First of all, back in the homeland, they generate not tens but *hundreds* of millions of pounds in takings. That money buys a lot of power, arms, foot soldiers, assassins, accountants, lawyers, businessmen, businesses, companies, properties, planes, ships, whatever. They can buy up a months' worth of heroin production and flood a country with it at not much over cost, halve the usual street value, double the addicts and kill anyone who argues.

Can you imagine how little resistance these kind of people would face in taking over this little country's crime empires? They'll wipe them out in a day, mop up the blood, and have polish back on the floor by next morning.

The British police don't know; they haven't the slightest. Haven't the fucking foggiest idea what could hit them. They're too busy running around chasing Yardies. They're wasting millions on nicking people who do a bit of weed. Four million it cost the Met to organise a massive raid in 1999 on a drugs house in London where they found a few Ks of weed. I know someone who could've sold them that amount for about one thousandth the cost!

The Yugoslavian geezer I mentioned in the chapter 'Weapon of Choice' who shot at the two British coppers without a second thought . . . that's what it would be like if they decided. The police in this country have never been to war. They think that's what the army do. But the police in Russia go to war every fucking day.

By looking at the profession I was in and knowing the signs, I can tell you it is as sure as eggs is eggs. They've looked over our little wall like a load of fucking hungry tigers looking into a school playground and thought, Yeah, we'll have some of that. Strategically planned. They've come out of Russia with their millions and millions.

The most exclusive and expensive shops in London which once relied on Arabs now give the majority of business to Russians. As do Mercedes, Lexus, Ferrari and Rolls-Royce when they start exporting. I've got friends that work on the Stock Exchange and for some of the biggest estate agents and they've told me how they've had Russian clients with bricks of cash buying up blocks of flats, businesses, hotels, streets. In the hotels they employ another 60 of their own. Buy an old school, turn it into a Russian language school with board and lodging, fill it up.

It's still very Us and Them with the Russian mob. It's bred into them. The Cold War is officially over but there's a lot of fucking thawing out to do and we probably won't live to see it.

And when the time comes they will say – to whoever the British crime lords are – 'You will not want a war with us: the closer we get to you you can see what we are and you will not want a war, and you will not mind being told what to do.' The clever ones will agree, the other clever ones will get out, and the rest will get disappeared. You either join them or retire. They ain't gonna play war games with London gangsters. We don't have wars. They've grown up in the middle of civil wars and city gangster wars.

They've been coming over here for years and then going back home with the message – You're not going to believe this . . . the policemen are *that* small, that young, and they're not even armed! And the gangs don't even use car bombs! And the company directors don't even wear bulletproof vests or have bodyguards! And they've never even had a Prime Minister killed!

I'm telling ya, we are here to be took. And I'm *fucking* glad I'm out of it. 'Cos having to try and learn to do that low-down Cossack dance is gonna be fucking murder on your legs.

14 DFATH BY CHOCOLATE (AND OTHER WAYS)

Listen to these tales I've got to tell you; these will wobble you a bit.

I've got a mate called JJ who's a muralist. No, I didn't know what it was either till I met him. He paints murals. After I moved into my house, Camelot Castle, I just happened to have a 60-foot, 3-floor-high gable-end wall that needed filling with a mural. It needed a fucking good muralling! Not something *I* do but, like I say, I know a man who does. Touch.

So along comes JJ with another mate Steve and a week later there was this massive and abso-fucking-lutely fantastic mural of me as Sir Lancelot on the back of a white charger with Jenny riding pillion as my queen. It is the absolute bollocks, mate. Which you'll already know if you've seen it. God's honest truth, cars crash outside because of people rubber-necking to get a better look at it. Especially at night when it's floodlit!

So just when the neighbours thought it was safe to come out the front door, and just when they probably thought nothing else more outrageous could be put on the house . . . out they come the next morning to see – da-*dah!* – this huge painting of me in armour; and my massive blue eyes staring down at them as they drive down the road! Imagine them filling your rearview mirror.

God knows what the neighbours did think, though. And you know what, if I gave a fuck I'd probably give a fuck.

Actually, come to think of it, I did give a fuck enough to post a letter to all my neighbours when I first moved in:

Hello

I am your new neighbour, Dave Courtney, and myself and my family are now living in number 18 ('Camelot', as it's now called) and I have no intentions of moving. This house is actually my dream house and I've been interested in it for many years.

I regret to inform you that my friends and family, work colleagues, cab drivers and, unfortunately, neighbours, are all subject to harassment by police and reporters, which I am sure you agree is an intrusion of our privacy.

I'm in the process of taking the police to court for harassment because this constant surveillance that myself and everybody I have contact with is very embarrassing for me. You or one of your immediate neighbours will be approached shortly, if not already, by one of these people and be asked for juicy gossip or maybe asked to allow cameras in your house to film me, or to befriend me and find out what I am up to. Well, I will tell you – I am writing a book, making a film – oh, yes, I have also got a magazine column and my latest venture is boxing promotions.

Unfortunately, because I refuse to drop my friends from my shadier past, the police and media refuse to accept the fact that I am no longer a villain myself. Please feel free to contact me at any time on my home phone number 0181 XXX XXXX if you have any problems with these people, or with my car being in the way or any other neighbourly advice you may feel is necessary. Don't waste your time coming to ask to borrow the lawn mower 'cos I haven't got one yet – so if anyone knows where I can get hold of a good cheap one I would be very interested, nudge, nudge, wink, wink. I would like to also take this opportunity to apologise to the person I offended by pruning my trees!

Thank you for your time. Your friend and neighbour,

Dave

P. S. Keep your eyes on the motor for us! Thank you.

There we go, that didn't scare anyone. I thought it was very welcoming. Nobody got a bloody mower for me though.

Anyway, back to the story; the thing is, before he went round brightening up my house with murals and destroying the neighbourhood property values, JJ was a police photographer up in Northumberland where he lives. Northumberland? Yeah, I know, don't fucking ask. It's somewhere up there in that northerny, countrysidey, no-neck-of-the-woods bit of Britain where they marry their mums, rape fish and eat their own toes for dinner. Bus service is once every full moon. They do a fucking good sausage though. No, no jokes. They just do a good sausage.

JJ weren't a copper but he got the call-out to all the crimes and accidents and deaths to record them. He saw some fucking freaky stuff, mate.

One time he got called out to a really weird one. He got to the house and found the local bobby stood there in the kitchen looking down at something and scratching his head (which ain't easy to do when you've still got your helmet on). Behind the door was this geezer that'd hanged himself with a belt, and on the floor was this wheelchair on its side and loads and loads of melted chocolate gateau all round it!

Go on then, solve that one then, Inspector fucking Morse . . .

For the answer ring my premium phoneline, 0870 007007, it's only £52.50 per minute. Calls should last no longer than two hours 'cos I recorded it when I was buzzing madder than a wasp in a bottle. Please ask whoever pays the bill to fuck off and mind their own business. Thank you.

No, what it was was this; this is what they finally worked out had happened. This geezer, who was dying of cancer, had decided to top himself. He was confined to a wheelchair, so maybe he's just got tired of being pushed around. Boom boom. But being in a wheelchair he realised he didn't have far enough to fall to hang himself, so he wheeled himself into the kitchen. His freezer was well stocked up 'cos his shopping was all done for him and there was loads of food stocked up in advance. And there was loads of boxes of his favourite sweet – chocolate gateau.

So he started shoving these boxes of gateau under his arse, one at a time, until he got higher and higher. High enough to hang himself. Then he threw a leather belt over a big hook on the wall, put it round his neck and toppled himself off this pile of gateau boxes he was sat on.

Then the police were called out, and JJ to photograph it all. That's quite a creative way to get round the problem of doing yourself in though, innit? That fucker must've really wanted to leave earth badly. Or maybe it was just some gateau/food-fuck fetish that went wrong.

So by choosing something off the sweet trolley the geezer made sure that his death was very unsavoury.

Which reminds me. The police were called out to a Pizza Hut after this geezer's body was found there covered in mushrooms, tomatoes, onions, peppers, ham and cheese. The police said they weren't treating it as murder because it looked like the man had topped himself.

There was another fella he told me about who did a similar thing. This farmer. He sent his old lady out to the shops, then drank two bottles of whisky, sat on the edge of his bed, put a double-barrelled shotgun in his mouth and took both barrels. Now, the little cottage they lived in had really, really low ceilings, only just over six foot high, which is fucking low. So when JJ got there he said the whole of the ceiling was completely repainted with this geezer's head and brains. His body was laid on the floor and the whole of his head was blown off. All that was left was the top of his spine, his lower jaw, his tongue hanging out on his neck and, get *this*, both of his eyeballs on his fucking tongue! Jesus fucking Christ.

As JJ walked around the room taking pictures he said he could feel drops of blood and brains falling off the ceiling and hitting the back of his neck.

I think we can safely say that that wasn't one of those suicide attempts that they say is just 'a cry for help'.

Another one was this guy who had an illness that was gradually crippling him and he couldn't stand it no more so one night he went a mile and a half in his wheelchair, built up some speed and flung himself off a cliff. He fell into a tree growing out of the cliff. They found him weeks later. He'd got impaled through the leg and died up there. Loads of birds had got at him and eaten bits of him and built a nest inside his chest. His wheelchair was up the tree as well, like a shopping trolley.

OK, I'm on a Sick Death roll now so I'll throw a couple more at you to think about next time you have spaghetti bolognese.

Right, this bloke lived local and he was a bit strange 'cos he had a fetish for really short women. He was about five ten, this bloke, but his wife was only just over four foot tall. So she was only a foot longer than a yard! Anyway, he'd also been caught messing about with this young schoolgirl and her father got hold of him and broke both his legs. Which I thought showed a lot of restraint, myself. He knew he was gonna get charged over the girl and he also knew he'⃝ get sent down, so he topped himself.

They found him in the front room stark bollock naked (apart from the two casts on his legs) with his feet in a washing-up bowl o⃝ water and wires wrapped round his hands. He'd ripped the flex of⃝ a lamp, plugged it in, wrapped the bare wires round his hands an⃝ then stood in the water. He flicked the plug switch on with ⃝ broomhandle! Very creative. Then it was Kentucky Fried Human⃝ He'd put his hands on his chest as he was cooking and the hea⃝ was so much it actually *melted* his hands into the muscles of hi⃝ chest.

They buried him on a baking tray.

This geezer who worked for Brendan on his building site got hi⃝ cock caught in the cement mixer while it was going round. He wa⃝ actually pissing in it, as a joke, pissing in the bucket mixer, then h⃝ started fucking about and got too close and it just whipped hi⃝ cock off! I heard about it when he came up to me months later ⃝ nice bloke as it happens – and he'd heard us talking about bein⃝ in the newspapers and he said, 'I was in the papers, Y'know. Yea⃝ I ripped my cock off.' I went, 'What?! You *what*?' Oh, we get som⃝ fucking funny ones come up to us, mate. When we go out we're lik⃝ a magnet for people with metal plates in their heads.

Just thought, do you remember the girl mentioned in *Raving Lunacy*, the one came up to us in a club and showed off the fact she only had nine toes? She'd had the other one cut off, and her boyfriend had kept it. Well, we bumped into her again recently, for the first time since then, and guess what? . . . She still had nine toes. I was surprised she had that many.

Listen to this one: talk about brain dead. This bloke decided he'd had enough (another one) so how did he decide to top himself — gas? bullet? noose? No, this fucker decided to *drill* himself to death. You'd think just the sound of that would make you come to your senses and carry on living, wouldn't you? So, he'd got one of those post drills — y'know the ones that are fastened to a bench and you pull it down — out in his garage. He stuck his head under and started pulling the bit down into his head.

When they found the body they wondered why there was blood trails from the garage into the house and back again, and pills on the floor. What they figured had happened was that after pulling the drill into his head a few times he decided it fucking hurt a bit — surprise, surpise — so he went into the house, swallowed some paracetamol for pain relief (true!) and then went back into the garage and drilled his head through. They found him pinned to the bench by the drill with a three-eighths bit stuck in his skull.

Wise move taking the pain killers, though. Could've been nasty otherwise. You think it would've been easier just to swallow all the pills in the first place, wouldn't you. Some people will do anything for attention.

Pretty fucking creative these ways, though, don't you think? Made me wonder why they didn't just go for the old gassing-yourself-in-the-car routine, y'know. At least it'd be painless. Did you know that after about three minutes the exhaust gas paralyses you physically, even though you're still awake. So if you change your mind after three minutes you are *fucked*, mate. And it does happen. JJ told me that a few of these car-gassing suicide merchants actually put video cameras on the dashboard to record themselves dying. He'd seen the films. Some of them start saying they've changed their minds and they don't want to carry on with it, but by then they can't move so they just have to die. That's what you call a proper video nasty.

Another weird one was a near-miss of someone I know. He lived out in the country and his dad ran a farm. When his old man bought a brand-new combine harvester my mate did the thing he usually did and sat right on top of it as his dad drove it. But both of them didn't take into account that the new machine was a good deal taller than the old one and the geezer sat on top got hit by some low power cables. There was a massive fuck-off bang as however many thousands and thousands of volts went through him, stopped his heart dead, and threw him burnt arse over black elbow into the air. He was dead then, technically, until he hit the floor. But he hit the ground so hard it actually jump-started his heart again!

His old man managed to get him to hospital and he recovered, but even now he still has an irregular heartbeat (fucking lucky he's got one at all I'd say!) and these big discoloured burnt patches on his skin where the electricity charge went in and out of his body.

And to this day he still can't bring himself to eat cornflakes.

15 EVERY STITCH AND STAB WOUND

I got introduced on a TV programme once as someone who had been stabbed, shot, burnt, punched, kicked and bottled. I had to say, 'Hold it! Wait a minute. I have actually *won* a few, you know!' Fuck me, they made me sound like a punchbag with 'Shoot Me' tattooed on my forehead. But then we're not here to talk about what I've inflicted on other people, even if it was sometimes for their own good; 'cruel to be kind' and all that.

I have, in my time, been in quite a few rucks, rumbles, rows, battles, wars, kick-offs and right proper tear-ups. And that's just with my mum and my missus. My mum was one of something mental like 16 children so she grew up learning how to fight for her porridge, 'know what I mean? So when I was a kid and I got a clump, it came from my mum not my dad 'cos she hit harder! And stone me, has my Jennifer got a good right hand or what? Left ain't too bad either.

So, anyway, along the way and over the years I've picked up a few tell-tale signs that suggest to people I'm not actually a celibate vegetarian Hare Krishna monk (although I have got some orange underpants, if that's close enough).

Well, you know how it is when you've been shot at, bitten and attacked with a meat cleaver. Worst of all, that was all when I was still a dustman. Fuck me, that was a tough round. It was because of that particular area that they brought out wheelie bins — ordinary dustbins just weren't big enough to get a body in.

All these battle scars and war wounds you pick up along the way during doorwork, debt collecting and just general all-purpose naughtiness. It's a hazard of the job and I can't say that you sometimes don't wear them with a little pride in the fact that you've survived. It's not 'til you sit down and count them that you see how many of the little bastards you've actually got. Every stitch and stab wound tells a story.

I think that's why I didn't even get past the audition stage to be a presenter for *Blue Peter*. Just a thought.

HEAD: Bit of a patchwork quilt is my old head. In fact it's got more stitches than Pavarotti's underpants. Once I went on a debt collection with Tucker, Mark and Milton Keynes Rob in, funnily enough, Milton Keynes. This geezer we was going to see was supposedly a bit of a handful and when he opened the door it looked like he was. We followed him into the kitchen, supposedly to talk, but I saw he was edging over to this board full of knives so I jumped on him. He called out then and this dirty great fucking Jurassic Park of a fuck-off American pit bull terrier came screaming into the room — fangs blazing! Mark, who just happened to have a baseball bat on him, bless him, hit this beast smack-bang on the bunce and completely flattened the fucker. Spark out. And thank fuck he did because he only had the chance for one shot before it would've had a snack attack on someone's bollocks. Meanwhile, I'm holding the geezer against the wall trying to stop him getting a knife and Mark comes up behind me and launches a right-hander at him over my shoulder. Unfortunately I moved my head to one side — the wrong one! — and *bam!* he hit the back of my head. I woke up God knows how long after . . . about February, I think; and it was a case of knit 1, pearl 2 down at the hospital Head Stitch Unit. Even now I've still got an 'I'-shaped scar on my head where one of the letters off Mark's initial ring embedded in my head. And the pit bull has a very flat head.

Another time me and Big Marcus came out of the Deja Vu club in Swanlea (funny, but it was always one of those clubs you felt like you'd been to before . . .) and saw these geezers breaking into my Jag. I jumped in the back seat just as they pulled away. One of them battered me with my own fucking Crooklock, but only until I got upright and smacked him out. Then the cunt driving crashed, and my head got another few bumps.

Down at Queens, the old club down by Heathrow I used to do the security for, I learnt a good one when this geezer swung a fire extinguisher round by the hose as a weapon. Unfortunately I was the one that ended up stopping it with my fucking head, but I did keep it in mind for when I used it in a crowd situation later on. This bloke was out of reach from me so I used the extinguisher trick and knocked him out from about six feet away! It was like having a massive metal conker.

The massive scrap I told you about in *Raving Lunacy* where we crashed a jeep in Spain and got mobbed by local gypsies, that left me battered and bruised all over, including the head. The coppers giving it to me in the nick afterwards didn't help either.

Come to mention it, I have rather carelessly thrown my skull against policemen's nightsticks many times. It was all my fault, obviously. I should've been more careful, all those times I've been handcuffed and held on the floor, not to let my head hit the copper's toecap time and time again. Yeah, the sneaky beating is alive and well: that old 'resisting arrest' line we know and love is still Top of the Cops.

I must have a naturally hard old head though 'cos I'm still standing. And don't that piss the people off who have tried to put you down.

EYE: Still got a scar from years ago when I got trapped between two buses outside the Cystal Palace Hotel nightclub and got beaten with those kung fu sticks — you know, the rice flail things that Bruce Lee uses? I've never eaten Chinese since. Although I have done the odd take-away.

NOSE: Had it broke twice, not a bad tally considering. Once in a street fight outside the Railway Signal pub. That was the place that me, my brother Patrick and our mates were in the night of the Chinese waiter swordfight I talk about in *Stop the Ride*. The other nose bending I got was in the boxing ring. And that was the last time I tried to jump over the ropes. It only works if you weigh 2st 6oz like Prince Naseem.

The Spanish gypsy war took its toll as well 'cos those fuckers stuck their fingers up my nose and tried to rip it open! Must be a fighting technique of theirs. A right bunch of Jack the Noserippers.

The worst thing that happened to my hooter was the end of it getting bit off in that infamous Old Kent Road bare-knuckle fight I had. Pulling his eye out was the least I could do in return. That got me on the front page of the *Sun* with a bandage across my face. My mum was so proud.

KNUCKLES: It has been reported that I've broken every knuckle on both hands. That ain't exactly true. I've broken no knuckles on either hand. Slight difference. That's where the knuckleduster comes in: it's like an airbag for your knuckles. Or in-flight protection when you've just launched a right-hander.

BACK: I've been stabbed in the back a couple of times in big crowd rows; while you're rolling around on the floor with a geezer, another one does you. What you might have heard about not realising you've been plunged, is true. You feel the hand that follows it in and think you've been punched; it disguises the stab. Also, years ago, when the football hooligan scene was at its height, I did the security at Millwall Social Club. Now don't that sound like an easy gig! Even the lightbulbs had little cages round them. It was the end of the football violence season but they were all still up for it and this massive row broke out in there. Darts were a popular weapon at the time and they started flying round like medieval fucking arrows. I got so many arrows stuck in my back I felt like I'd been given acupuncture by King Kong.

Luckily no one got the bullseye – so I could still sit down.

EAR: I didn't need that little wiggly bit on the side of my ear anyway. Good job 'cos some cunt bit it off. He did get paid back double though.

RIGHT ARM: I got a knife stuck into me by a gypsy. It got jammed in the elbow bone joint and just stuck there! Even I thought, *wow*. So next time a gypsy asks you if you want to buy some lucky heather, say yes.

RIGHT HAND: These little piggies of mine nearly didn't go to market when my fingers got cut with a cleaver during the Chinese sword-fight. Not a bundle of laughs that night, was it really? But a funny one that did happen was when this fella suspected that I was shagging his missus, which I was. We used to go wrestling together, me and this bloke, and this time he invited me to go prac-tise in his back yard. Fair enough. When we started wrestling, though, he went mad, threw me all over the bleedin' place for about fifteen minutes and broke two of my fingers! After that I *knew* that *he* knew about his missus and me, and that was his way of getting me for it, but I couldn't exactly *say* anything about it, could I?

LEFT ARM: I was involved in a mass tear-up years ago when this bloke pulled out a flick knife and threw it at me. I think he was as totally gobsmacked as me when the blade actually stuck in my fucking arm! So was everybody else 'cos they all stopped fighting and looked. Again, even I had to give a little *wow* at seeing it stuck out there. It was one of them things you don't think happens outside of films. The only thing missing was a commentator shout-ing, One hundred aaannd *eighhhh-teee!* Anyway, thank fuck the geezer didn't pull out another and go for double top.

CHEST: I was doing the door one New Year's Eve at this bar. It was nearly full and no sign of anyone else coming so the other doormen were inside. This bloke came up to the door by himself so I told him it was couples-only night. I don't know how many places he'd already been turned away from but he suddenly flipped and went beserk. He was a big bodybuilding fucker as well, so when he grabbed me there weren't a lot I could do. He chucked me on to this parked car and pinned me there, back to the roof, with him holding me down by my elbows. I could only move enough to do little hits on his head. He couldn't punch me 'cos he didn't want to let go of my arms so he just started ripping through my clothes with his teeth and then biting my fucking chest! Like an animal.

I'd already dropped my duster at my feet. There was this lady called Karen that had been talking to me at the door when this kicked off. Karen was slim and absolutely, strikingly beautiful, wearing a mini skirt and stilletto heels. She was like Betty Boo, the cartoon babe. So I'm pinned to this car, this mad geezer's trying to fucking eat me, and I saw Karen come *tottering* over! She picked up my duster between two fingers and in her little voice said, 'Here y'are!' and slipped it on my hand like a vicar puts on a wedding ring; it was just like that. Then she tottered away. I could *ding* him on the head then, little hits but with the duster on I could feel him sagging. Then I got my arm free and gave him a *proper* fucking smack.

When you nearly lose one, like I was losing that one, but then manage to turn it around, you know you have to finish the guy off, and I completely battered him. And a happy new year to you too.

RIBS: I was selling a bullet-proof vest and decided to show off and test it to help the sale along. I put it on but the blokes with me didn't want to shoot the gun in case something went wrong and they ended up on a murder charge. My mate Ian Tucker seized the opportunity to shoot me and get away with it! So he fired a slug into the vest and it fucking hurt 'cos I felt a rib snap. The vest worked though but we had to chuck it 'cos it now had a hole in it! It was like the old joke about the Irish geezer striking matches to see if they're duds or not. Any road, I got further orders for vests but it weren't worth a snapped rib.

One night, me, my pal Colin Robinson and my brother Patrick went out on the rob. Pat was a good bit younger than me but even at his age he was a game little fella, and I knew he'd grow up to be an even handier man. On this coup, though, he was lookout. We broke into Finchies store. It sold anything and everything, which is exactly what we were after. On one of the shelves was this gold, antique money till, one of those old-fashioned ones with big buttons and 'five shilling' signs. Gotta be worth a bob or two, so Colin threw it to me. In the dark I thought it was bigger than it was and opened my arms too wide. The till hit me corner-first smack in the ribs. *Crack!* That was over twenty years ago and I can still feel it now when I think about it.

Patrick grew up to be a brother to be proud of. It ain't always been a plus in life to have me as a brother, I know that, so in *Stop the Ride I Want to Get Off* I didn't mention Pat too much so as to protect him. 'Cos he's a proper straight goer, my bro, and some people I don't want to drag into my books just to make an exciting story. Patrick was there during a lot of them, though. He could tell you a few tales of his own. He ain't been 'little Patrick' for years now, of course, not since we were kids; in fact he's a bit of a secret weapon. Imagine having a younger brother who's not as well known as you but twice as handy. Touch.

Patrick was also beside me all the way through Ronnie Kray's funeral and who better to have by your side on a day like that than your own brother.

ARSE: Yeah, I got stabbed in my fucking arse! It was a proper pain in one as well. The padding helps though. Thank fuck I weren't Frankie Fraser's height 'cos in my position he'd have got it in the face. Not that I'm saying my arse and his face have anything in common. For one thing, no one wants to smack my arse! And no one says his face is a peach! *Bum bum.*

Anyway, it was another one of those cases of feeling like you've just been punched or kicked, rather than stabbed, until your mates point out your arse is actually squirting blood everywhere. Oh, the glamour of crime. That's the side of it they don't show you in the movies – *Lock, Stock and Two Punctured Arse Cheeks*! And you know when you hurt your leg and get a 'dead leg'? Well, I got a 'dead arse', mate. I could've sat on a hedgehog with a hard-on and not felt it. Which is a bit worrying, 'cos maybe I did.

RIGHT KNEE: In a geezer called Tony's place, 'Lollipop' in Windmill Street, I got shot in the knee; but fortunately it was only a .22 gun, so I just got a bit of metal stuck in me instead of losing half my leg. But like my mum used to say to me, 'Don't come running to me when you break your legs!'

When I was doing the security at the Connaught Rooms thousands of people turned up there for an audition. This one big black geezer pushed to the front of the queue, started mouthing off at security and then started stomping up the steps towards me. I did the old 'punch to the belly to double him up' trick, which is always followed by a knee to the chops. Trouble is this cunt mistook my knee for a chop and clamped his teeth around it as I brought me knee up. Fuck me, it hurt, it really does when you get bit. Absolute agony. He got dragged off and knocked out but not before he'd drawn blood.

Turns out the geezer was a former copper on the run from Africa! So I had to have an Aids test, tetanus injections, rabies jabs, the lot. So I've even been bitten by the Old Bill, and one that travelled thousands of miles to do it. Cheers.

LEFT LEG: This is where I got shot in the shin by a 9 milli Luger. The cunt was obviously going for more but that's all he got when I took some action. The 'action' being of the 'jumping out the way over parked cars' kind of action. Any other reaction in the face of someone trying to shoot you seems pretty fucking dopey to me. It's not like it's the perfect way to round off a night out, is it? – drink with mates, go for curry, dance in club, pull bird, get shot in head, bleed in taxi. So if you end up in a situation where you're unarmed and some fucker's trying to get a bead on you, just put one foot in front of the other as quickly as possible. It's an old trick called being smart and *running*.

16 MEET THE CHAPS

Times have changed and so have the people. Now most crime means drugs, and most of the old-school don't dabble in that at all. To be a higher echelon naughty person, or 'alternative businessman' (to use a phrase I've just made up), you don't need to be a blinding fighter or a crack shot and all that — what you have to be is a very, very, very good judge of character. That's the one attribute that serves you best, believe me. It ain't the flashiest thing in your armoury but it's the biggest life-saver you've got. That judgement is the thing that you have to keep bang-on every time.

It was while I was boxing as a kid at the Honor Oak gym in Forest Hill that I first saw, up close, the known chaps and faces from the streets. The kind of fellas that everybody knew about and everybody wanted to know, or be like. They were proper men, men's men, and they had character and an inner confidence in their own ability that just oozed out of them, and most people don't have that. You have to have that. People can spot weakness so you have to know that you are very good, the best or very close to it:

LENNY McLEAN

I've seen a lot of hard men and fighters, but he was the godfather. He was a proper fighting machine. Thank fuck we never had to fight, but I did spar with him a few times, and came second every time. He will be a very, very hard act to follow, will Lenny, and a fucking huge pair of boots to fill.

But there was a real man behind what became the myth, as there always is. Lenny was originally a window-cleaner and bouncer. Not many people remember that he started out fighting as Lenny 'Daddy Cool' McLean, before he became The Guv'nor, in bouts like the grudge match he had with a car-breaker called Cliff 'Iron Man' Fields in Finsbury Park. There was an awful lot of London's top villainy there that night. Fields came out on top that time and knocked out Lenny in the fourth.

That was quite rare though 'cos he was a formidable presence. When I was younger it was at Honor Oak Boxing Club, the Thomas à Becket gym, the Lin Boxing Club, Fisher Boxing Club and also at Peckham Boys that I first saw the famous unlicensed boxers like Lenny, Roy Shaw, Fred the Head, Harry Starbuck, Teddy Webb and Columbo. Each one looked like they could tear off your arm and smoke it, just to pass the time! I later went on to fight on the under-cards at some of these fellas' main bouts.

Later still me and Lenny ended up working together on jobs, door-work and debt collections. One time this geezer took one look at Lenny and started shouting 'Call the police!' Lenny went, 'Order a fucking ambulance while you're at it!' The geezer fainted on the spot and we just wet ourselves laughing.

He weren't the best technical fighter but then he usually didn't give the other geezer time to use any technique either. He certainly learned to make the most of himself, did Lenny, and played to his strengths. That's a valuable one to learn, right there — play to your strengths, and quietly try to eradicate your weaknesses.

On another debt collection job we were outnumbered in a car scrapyard but Lenny decked a couple of the geezers straight off. 'There,' he said, 'that evens things up a bit!'

The way he went, eventually, the way he died through cancer, is an awful, awful way to go. A nasty way for a man to go — for a big, proper man like Lenny. It's not exactly a straightener either, fighting cancer. A fair crack of the whip don't come into it. And for a big man to have to see yourself waste away like that . . . He proves something I knew to be true when I started going down this new road of mine; that even when you go your book can live on and on. You can still be on the shelves when even the great, great, great grandsons of the worms that originally ate you are dead!

I feel honoured to have been a friend of Lenny's.

ROY 'PRETTY BOY' SHAW

Roy is another legendary figure and was a top unlicensed fighter. A bit of a feud and rivalry started between Roy and Lenny, in the ring anyway, because Roy was thought of as the top fighter and the man you had to beat. They fought three times and took one apiece until they had a decider. That was the most famous bout between them and was caught on film at the Rainbow Theatre, Finsbury Park. Whenever you see some documentary on unlicensed fighting and how brutal it is, that film of Roy and Lenny is always the one they show to prove it! What a compliment.

Roy was a real all-rounder, though — he did banks, building societies, Securicor vans, the lot. He got a fifteen sentence for one job but didn't do his time quietly, as you might expect. His prison antics were legendary as well. He once did a bit of DIY redecoration and knocked down a cell wall with a pool table. Fucking hell, you don't get that on *Changing Rooms*!

And talking about when we were in Brazil, what people might not know about Roy is that he's a fantastic singer — I've heard his 'Two old ladies sitting in the sand, each one wishing the other was a man . . .' We also saw him dispose of a cigarette in the most unusual way. All in all he's an all-round party animal: a glass-eating, bottle-smashing, all-punching, all-singing and dancing party monster.

The dressing gown that he used to wear in the ring had 'The Mean Machine' written across the back. That was the name of a film that was popular at the time, and one of my favourite films, about a group of American cons that play a football match against the screws and completely batter them. One film you never got to see in prison, funnily enough! I list it on the end credits of *Hell to Pay* as one of my inspirations.

Anyway, Roy was the mean machine of his day. I'm also very proud to say Roy is a friend. I gave him a bulletproof vest on one of his birthdays and he said he appreciated it because when he was younger they just used to bounce off!

FREDDIE FOREMAN

Fred's nickname during the Kray days was The Undertaker, so enough said. He's real old-school, from the original era. He was one of those that showed it could be done in a dignified manner.

During Ron Kray's funeral four of the pallbearers of the casket were chosen to represent different areas of London. East End was Charlie Kray, West was Teddy Dennis, North was Johnny Nash and the South was represented by Fred himself. That all the manors came together on one day was a tribute to Ronnie.

Personally, I think Freddie Foreman's autobiography, *Respect*, is the best of all the crime books. Fred is looked upon as the jewel in the crown by everyone in the business.

JOEY PYLE

Another older premier division. Joe's been promoting boxing since the sixties. He managed Roy Shaw and was the one mostly responsible for the unlicensed bouts taking off in London. He was one of the fellas that I'd admire when they came in the gym. Later on came to know him and learn from him. He still fucking tells me off up to today, and if I needed a clump over something he wouldn't be too shy to give it.

The wedding of Joey Pyle's son, Joe junior, in 1998 was the classiest, most spare-no-expense wedding I've ever been to or heard about in my life. It was in Boxley Hill on the land of Eddie Cox. There was a trout lake there, and all these big marquees, spit roasts cooking lamb, and it was a beautiful sunny day.

Every single, solitary face that you could possibly imagine that could be called 'connected', was there. Every single one, going right back. Lenny McLean didn't make it because he was ill and he didn't want to be seen ill obviously. All the British lot and even some of the Italians over from the States came. It was a real honour to be at.

Joe senior was walking around in his white tuxedo and everyone was bow-tied up. There was free Bollinger, bottles and bottles of it in ice buckets, and ice sparkling everywhere. There were even ice sculptures. There must have been a thousand people. It was like something you'd imagine a Hollywood star to have. It was a fucking amazing sight. There was quite a few celebs there. When it's for show the fellas don't mind the celebrities being there.

A live band played all day and during the evening the Drifters played a set.

A funny thing that happened was that this geezer came out of prison on home leave on the very morning of the wedding and came along. He knew them all. He said it was really weird for him 'cos he knew them all when he went away twenty-some years ago, and the day he comes out here they all are, but 60, 65 and 70 years old! Everyone a bit fatter or greyer or balder than they were before, but still there. How freaky must that have been for him?

What a fucking day to come out though.

RONNIE BIGGS

Ronnie is the most famous of the Great Train Robbers, not because he was the brains of it but 'cos he escaped and stayed escaped the longest. The fact that they've actually brought him home and whether he'll still be alive when this book comes out, I don't know, but I think it is awfully sad that everyone couldn't do more for him out there. And only someone who had been away from Britain for so long would think you could come back here and get quick treatment on the NHS. I'm all for coming home to end your days but better to do it free on a Brazilian beach.

Ronnie was the one that escaped from Wandsworth Prison, and whether he was or wasn't a star when he arrived in Brazil he definitely played the British on-the-run star criminal for all it was worth. I went out to see him on his seventieth birthday and Ronnie was the perfect Englishman abroad. He played the superstar very, very well and I applaud him for that. I had one of the best weeks of my life when I went to his house and I'll never forget it.

For me it was the equivalent of meeting someone like Muhammad Ali, especially for someone who likes to knock authority a bit; he was the one who kicked them *right* up the fucking arse and gave a million people a light at the end of the tunnel. Personally, I think that the only reason they brought him or encouraged him to come back was to take away a lot of other people's lights at the end of their tunnels, 'cos Ronnie was the great, famous escaper who then did the classic thing of turning up on a beach in the sun thousands of miles away! What a fucking dream that is to everyone inside doing bird or stuck in a dead-end job.

In my eyes he's still a superstar, and his son Mickey Biggs is a fucking lovely geezer as well. I had the privilege of meeting him out there and he's since come and stayed at my house. We did a little cheeky scene in my film *Hell to Pay* where I had Mickey playing a screw in Wandsworth, the nick his old man escaped from. He looks into a cell and says, 'Sorry, lads, I've got to go. I'm late for a train!'

Mickey's a talented lad but he's also paying the price for having a famous criminal dad.

BRUCE REYNOLDS

Bruce is, I think, who Michael Caine modelled himself on. And not a lot of people know that. Michael Caine knew he weren't ever going to bump into Bruce 'cos he was doing time.

He was the brains behind the Great Train Robbery – another sign of times long gone because it was an era of men all clubbing together and pulling together and getting a little job done; just like they were trained to do in the army during National Service.

Now, forty years down the line, everybody's freelance and pulling their own way, but back then it was quite easy for groups of men to join together and get a job done with precision and planning. I applaud the brain work it must have taken to sort out the plan. Bruce is another one that came out to Brazil for Ronnie's party.

He must be the most all round intellectual man I've met; and he has got such a charming, intelligent way of speaking that you just feel embarassed to breathe, and his book about his life is, as you'd expect, blinding.

THE KRAYS

I took it as an honour to be asked to organise Ronnie Kray's funeral. At the time I saw it as a good career move but the opposite happened 'cos it held me up in front of the public. The police put me down as 'a Kray twin gang member' or 'heir to the Krays', when really when they were running round Bethnal Green all those years ago I was still in my pram chucking rusks at everyone.

To be honest, the closer I got and the more I got to know about the Krays the less impressed I was, I'm afraid. They were not the actual guv'nors of that era; it was quite obvious that it was the Richardsons. The twins were the ones that clambered more for the press and fame thing, which I suppose I am also guilty of; but I'm also not trying to say that I'm the tastiest thing since sliced bread.

I met them when they'd already been in prison for a very long time, at the tail end. I never really met the two geezers that the myth had been built around . . . 'cos when I met them they'd both been living in boxes for twenty years. I could not say, with my hand on my heart, that they were the most intelligent human beings in the world but they were obviously a force in their heyday.

They definitely considered kindness as a weakness. I wasn't, by the end of their time, a Kray twin fan, really. I admired what they'd stood for, they'd ruled their patch, and they did their time; and I take my hat off to anyone who can do that amount of bird and still be there mentally. But Reg lost all the gift of being able to read people as a result of being locked up with one certain type, and also lost all sense of reality, which took some of the shine off the legend for me. But there was a time when I was just as impressed as everyone else to have met him.

Times change, and especially quickly for those with short memories. It was a lot easier to rule Bethnal Green 35 years ago when there was only 30,000 people there, whereas now there's probably 230,000 and a lot of them can't speak English: they wouldn't listen to two tasty geezers who owned the snooker hall down the road *whoever* they were. That's just fact, although I'm not judging them on how they were then because I only met them after they'd been in prison and were long past being legendary figures.

The public were led to believe that myth mostly by the authorities so they could justify what was, without a fucking shadow of doubt, a miscarriage of justice to keep them banged up until they died. But the twins also partly encouraged that myth-making thing and I don't think they realised how it would be used against them until it was too late.

My theory is that it's nice to be important but it's important to be nice. I motivate people in a completely different way to the one the twins did. Their mistake was this, that they seemed to think they could run an empire on fear. That is a recipe for disaster from the moment you even *begin* thinking that way. You should expect people to be loyal to you because they love you and 'cos they wouldn't want to see you go through pain. The Krays tried to do it on a different basis where the idea was: 'You do that or I'll hurt you.' But once you take away the threat of that, e.g., putting them both in prison, then everyone just buckles. Loyalty should grow from people *wanting* to be loyal.

Even the geezers who did stay loyal to them, like Chris and Tony Lambrianou, weren't repaid with the same. Chris and Tony, and a few others, carried the can and got sent down without saying anything. Then a few years later the twins wrote a book about it all, which meant that some of their firm had done time for nothing.

An awful lot of people that carried the myth along were people that never met them, and if you did for any long periods of time then you got to know the ins and outs and the truth behind the myths – as there is with every well-known character, including myself. No one can live up to a myth. But I'm afraid the closer I got to the real Kray twins the further away I wanted to be. I ended up with the burden of knowing things I wish I hadn't . . . I can't say no more than that, really. All the same, you've got to give Ronnie big respect for being strong enough to do that time and see his family die while he was still inside. It's just sad.

THE RICHARDSONS

The Richardsons, brothers Charlie and Eddie's firm, ruled south London with an even stronger iron fist than the Krays did over the river, but they did it with a mink glove on the outside. They were in the scrap business and were proper money-earners. They looked after their people an awful lot more than the Krays looked after theirs. There was an awful lot of the twins' behaviour that wouldn't have gone on in the Richardsons' camp. The way the twins' gang members were jumped on to take the blame, for instance; the Richardsons were more the type to lead from the front.

They were more into the pounds, shillings and pence of what they did than struck by the fame thing at all. They were professional at whatever they did whenever they did it.

I've met Charlie Richardson several times at different events and found him a very sharp geezer, a nice man to talk to but you could see that you would not want to fuck with him even today. I should imagine that the man's got one of the scariest filofaxes in the world.

FRANK FRASER

He was one of the first gentlemen I met. It was me that brought Frankie Fraser down to Maidstone Prison when there was a very memorable visit when a lot of the old guard – Charlie Richardson, Charlie Kray, Frankie Fraser, Alex Steen – all met up together while visiting Reggie Kray. It was the first time they'd all met in thirty years. Last time they had some of them were sworn enemies.

I helped orchestrate the meeting and took Frankie down there. To be honest, from the very first moment I met him I fucking loved the geezer to pieces. I was an awful lot younger then, though, but you could've put me down as a fan, and I'm not embarrassed to say that.

I would be embarrassed to say it now though because of things that have been said. I'm afraid I'm not the only one who's fallen foul of Frank as he also had a go at Freddie Foreman, which is fucking unbelievable. For a long time I resisted replying to Frank 'cos I just didn't want to get into some undignified squabble – and these things shouldn't really be done in public anyway – but it just got far too much. And as Fred himself said in the book he did with Tony

Lambrianou, *Getting it Straight*, 'a lie uncontradicted becomes accepted truth, so you can't ignore it'. Which I think is a very, very wise way indeed of looking at this kind of situation.

Frankie making comments about the colour of my missus not meeting his approval was the last straw with me, so that's why we obviously don't get on. But I don't have any personal axe to grind, and you can't help but take your hat off to someone who did that amount of bird and is still as lively and sprightly as he is. He'll probably live to be a hundred. And that prospect must please his wife.

I don't think he'll be getting a Christmas card off me this year though.

CHARLES BRONSON

Well, what can I say? You know Charles. The most frightening beard in the world. Britain's most infamous criminal. And what a singer! But he's also a nice fella, believe it or not, and another man who is gifted in many ways. He's also another one of those fellas that I think if the authorities gave him a chance he would be OK. But they are determined not to bend an inch where Charles is concerned.

I wish him all the happiness in his new marriage to Sara. I put on the wedding reception at the Manhattan Cafe where I had a drink with Lord Longford of all people. That was another event covered by the press where they carefully avoided mentioning me. They said everything about the reception apart from my involvement in it. Surprise, surprise.

Anyway, everyone had a good day on the day. I just hope Charlie don't decide he wants to honeymoon on the prison roof.

BIG ALBERT CHAPMAN

Big Al is a proper, *proper* one, in my eyes. I cannot put the man high enough. He's a big, six-foot-six Birmingham fella, for one thing, and you don't get much higher than that! But he's held in very high esteem. He's gone through the ranks and now owns a dog track, got his own music business, his own nightclub — The Elbow Rooms — and he's everybody's friend. I don't care who's fallen out with who, everyone gets on with Albert Chapman.

Everyone always turns up for his birthday. The last I went to they did a *This Is Your Life*-type surprise for him. I was up there with Freddie Foreman and Tony Lambrianou, and people came from everywhere 'cos the guy is the bollocks and they love him to bits.

WILF PINE

Wilf is a proper little workhorse for the firm. Well-respected member on both sides of the ocean and he's always got a hand to help out.

He's stood beside me at times where I truly needed some pals around me and for that I will always love him.

GEOFF THOMPSON

London faces grab an awful lot of the credit and the limelight 'cos the media is down here with us but there's people up and down the country who you might not hear about, or they might not want you to hear about them. You'll know Geoff by now though because he's probably written more books than the lot of us put together about his days on the door, and very good they are too.

He's definitely a force to be reckoned with is Geoff, and I wouldn't like to be on the bad side of him.

CAS PENNANT

Cas is another very, very tasty bastard; a very capable boxer and a man that understands loyalty and honour to the bone. Even though he's a well-known fighting man, he did fight with honour. He's known for his bravery and whether it was frowned upon where he decided to have his fights – at the football matches – it was definitely cheered on by the crowds.

BERNIE DAVIES: 'AGENT No 10'

Welsh Bernie has got to come under the class of 'one of the chaps'. You do not get harder than the pit men, the valley men. They have a bit of a soft spot up there for me — no, not the local swamp! — because while the miners strike was on and Margaret Thatcher was doing her best to rip the heart out of the country, I used to go up there once every two weeks with a Transit full of food. I'd collect it from doormen and council workers and I'd take whatever doormen I had with me for spares — normally about a dozen — and we'd go up there on a Friday night.

We'd arrive twelve-handed with our tools, drop off the food, and then go on the front line with the miners and help them beat up Old Bill. Perfect fucking holiday; I'd have paid for it!

They did actually say to me at the time that it was the first time anyone from England had driven up there to help them out, and they haven't forgotten it. And I haven't forgotten the awful, fucking catastrophic thing I saw when I was up there. It twisted my mind to feel that I had to be a voicepiece for the people to speak out at what the police can do to normal people and get away with it — and what I saw was coppers actually laying into not only the men but also their women and kids; just because they wanted somewhere to go to work. You had to see it to believe it, and if you see the end result when you have a look now, twenty years down the line, it is one of the saddest things you'll ever see — a ghost town on the side of a mountain which no one can earn enough money to get down off.

That's very sad and it breeds a very hardy person and I'm very proud to say that Welsh Bernie, my number 10, is what I consider one of the best chaps indeed, as are most of the people surrounding him.

IAN FREEMAN

Ian is the new phenomenon in the fight game in this country, I believe. Lenny McLean in his heyday and Roy Shaw in his would not beat Ian Freeman on his top form. Everything has changed over the last twenty years. The 100-metre sprint is faster now than it was then. We come from an era when Lenny was the hardest boxer and puncher and those two fighters stood there punching lumps out of each other. Well, Ian Freeman, and the modern freestyle fighters, do a completely different kind of scrapping.

Ian's method is called Vale Tudo — which is Portuguese for 'anything goes' — and it's a no-holds-barred fighting. From round one his sole intention would be to dive to the floor, grab your foot and break your ankle! Or pull your toes apart and cripple you. And I don't care how tasty a bastard you are you can't have a row while hopping on one fucking leg. Apart from anything else you'd look like a cunt.

Grappling is now the most vicious sport. They don't rely on planting one on the sweet spot on your chin, they just pull you down on the canvas and tie your arms in a knot behind your fucking head. Or get you in a hold that feels like your spine's gonna snap.

Ian fights in suspended cages against Russian geezers, stuff like that, proper out-there battles. You would *not* like to have a roll around on the floor with one of those big lumps.

He's also a funny bastard and I gave him a role in *Hell to Pay*, playing my cellmate.

The very first time I met Ian was when I was presenting him with a prize in the ring. He'd just had a vicious little fight with an American and I got in there with this plastic trophy and I said, 'You've just gone through all that for this?' In his Sunderland accent he went, 'I didn't do it for that, man. I just wanted to hurt the cunt!' I thought, Fucking hell, imagine living next door to *that*!

DAVE FORD

Dave was one of the most well-respected bank robbers this country's ever had. He was the Beckham of bank robbers. Which is probably why years ago the police took an out-and-out diabolical liberty with him and actually took millions of pounds' worth of art that legitimately belonged to Dave, and then on top of that threw him in prison.

He's now going through a court case that has taken seventeen years to overturn the judgment he was originally sentenced for. But he's worked out that the thousands of pounds' worth of interest per day that he's lost since 1984 means that the police owe him something like £39 million! So he's bringing a world record civil suit for that amount against the police. And 'cos the Old Bill now know what the financial burden of telling the truth will be they're trying to back out of it. There is even the police's own evidence with them admitting that serving officers involved in his case have already spent a million pounds of bearer bonds that were taken off him when he was arrested.

So the Met not only wrongly arrested him but then took his stuff off him *and* spent his money! Sir Paul Condon was in charge then and has been called to court over it but has decided not to turn up, which is actually contempt of court. Me and you would get done for that but guess what . . .? It looks like Sir Condom ain't particularly worried. Funny that.

Everybody's keeping everything crossed for Dave that things will work out as they should, and also hoping that this is one nest of snakes that's even too big for the Met to try and hide.

I recently went up to Sunderland to do an 'Audience with Dave Courtney' and to support my pal Ian Freeman who was launching his book. In the audience was a lady called Winnie Bennett, whose son Keith was a victim of Myra Hindley and Ian Brady, the Moors murderers. Keith's body was never found and his mother don't feel she can be at peace until her boy is laid to rest. Dave Ford came all the way up from London to promise a large donation of the money he will win to go towards the fund for the search on the moors for Keith Bennett's body.

Top geezer, Dave Ford.

EAMMON O'KEEFE

Not all chaps look or act like or even want to be one of the chaps, and they don't realise their importance to other people until they are not there. And because these people ain't the biggest, or loudest, or most flamboyant they sometimes might feel they are not the most important. Well, let me tell you there is a man called Eammon O'Keefe, and in my eyes he is one of the chaps. The fact that he's never robbed a bank, been on a firm or been inside, or anything like that, makes no difference 'cos this geezer's heart is as big as anyone's I've mentioned, and his loyalty, integrity and honesty are beyond question. His generosity knows no bounds, and Eammon, I fucking salute you!

WINSTON CHURCHILL

No, I'm *not* that old and I didn't actually know him, you cheeky astards, but he has *got* to be the biggest chap of all time. Or let's ay, at least, the biggest British chap; that way we don't offend the ig Holy chap upstairs.

ow wicked was it that his mum and dad gave him a dread name! eah, mon, Winston Churchill! Give me a 'W'!, give me an 'inston'!

n my eyes he was the ultimate man that proved it ain't all about aving the most muscles and all that in order to be in charge and natural leader. 'Cos this little short geezer actually said things hat mobilised a nation, that made a tiny little country like Britain hink they could get up and win a world war. So whatever it was he ould say to make this country get up and think, 'Right: I'll do every astard!' – well, that geezer deserves praise of the highest order or that. Most people couldn't motivate a chicken to cluck let alone whole country to have a row with a big chunk of the world.

e had a proper genius for finding the right words to make you well with pride – 'I have nothing to offer but blood, toil, tears nd sweat'; '. . . whatever the cost may be, we shall fight on the eaches, we shall fight in the fields and streets, we shall never urrender'; 'Never in the field of human conflict was so much wed by so many to so few'; 'Give us the tools, and we will finish he job'.

Every one an absolute peach. 'Give us the tools, and we will finis the job' . . . fucking *hell*! Every top naughty geezer I know would b proud of that! Churchill was a gutsy, spunky little geezer and think we should be proud to have had him.

Top cigar smoker, and chap of chaps.

7 THE FEMALE OF THE SPECIES

Now where women are concerned you've got all different types of qualities and all different types of hard. But I don't think anyone is under any illusion about which sex is the most deadly of the species. All those things my nan said are true, and hell hath no fury like a woman scorned. The lengths to which a woman will go never ceases to amaze a fella.

Look at one of the biggest tyrants of recent times, Margaret Thatcher. How much more horrible can you get than that one?

You can find women that are hard in the mind and stand solid with their husbands when their old man's in prison. He might have been there for ten, fifteen years and she still doesn't stray, and you can't get much harder than that; but she could still be an absolute perfect lady.

I actually know a couple that've got a punchbag up in their front room and every single morning the family have to come down and bash the fuck out of this bag! And the wife, without a shadow of a doubt, is the scary one of that family, believe me. She can do ten rounds on that bag when her old man only does one. So there's that kind of tough woman.

I know some Eastern European women who could look at you and give you a fucking orgasm, but they are actually trained killers, are crack shots and are up for sale for ten grand if you want to have someone popped off. But they look like fucking Heidi from the mountains, y'know, butter wouldn't melt.

It's a definite plus having women in some situations, plus they've got all the added extras that God gave them to get men running around doing what they want.

There's the women who make men fight for them. They'll go out of their way to get the best fighter and the man who likes fighting the most, and try and get him to fight all the time. There's birds that get off on that. As long as she's a good shag he'll carry on fighting till he's locked up. She's a danger to the fella and to his mates. In fact, he'll probably end up fighting his mates rather than hear a word against her. After all, you're only his friend; she's the one who sucks his dick every night. He ain't gonna side with you even if he should.

If one of those little, destructive, timebomb-women gets into your company then she can cause fucking havoc because you can't tell the man anything, you really can't. As much as your loyalty should be to your lady first — and prison teaches you your priorities where home life and family are concerned — it has to be one that's worth of that loyalty. Otherwise you just end up fucking off everybody else that's been there for you for someone else who won't be.

Women can be the making of you and the breaking of you. I've seen genuinely hard men cry about what to do when their marriage breaks up. Blokes inside that have had screws jumping up and down on their heads and been thrown in the punishment block, they'd rather go through that again than get the 'Dear John' letter from the missus.

Men will argue time and time again, and actually be more forgiving than women in many ways, but the way a woman only takes so much and then suddenly cuts off is a scary thing to most men. And most men don't see it coming until it's too late. The screaming and shouting you can stand 'cos you understand it, but when a woman very quietly says, 'Leave . . . that's it, I don't want you any more,' then you *know* you're fucked. Women put up with more, and for longer, than men do, but once they go from you emotionally . . . then that's it, mate.

And the women reading this know, as much as the men know, that that is true.

It's worthwhile having women door people, very much so. People are under the misconception that men are on the door 'cos they're good for a fight, and that used to be the case. But now when you can get nicked for even slapping someone you need a different tactic. Women can obviously deal with other women better. A bird wouldn't want some hairy-arse doorman looking through her handbag, or checking out the women's toilets or jumping between two girls fighting. I ain't saying some of them aren't handy though, 'cos some of the women I've met who work the doors would surprise you with what they could throw at you.

I saw Jane Couch, the British women's boxing champion, the other day. I sponsored a fight for Joey Pyle at the Wembley Conference Centre. Top of the bill was this geezer called Butterbean who's a massive 25½ stone American fighter. The ring canvas was covered with the name of my film *Hell to Pay*, but you could hardly see it for the two massive fuckers fighting at heavyweight! Anyway, Jane Couch the boxing lady was on the bill and you've got to see this woman fight. Put it this way, if there's a hormone thing in a man that can make him think he should have been a woman, then this woman must have that in reverse 'cos she can fucking fight like a man. I wouldn't want to be even in the same building if she was on her period.

Women, I think, deserve most of the applause, and when asked why there isn't a woman boss in the underworld I say there fucking well is. Because whoever you consider the bosses, behind them are the wives telling them, and rightly so! We the men need the brakes putting on us and they, the women, are the only ones to do so. The only honest criticism you're gonna get from anyone is from your mum and your missus 'cos they are the only ones that are in it for no personal gain. They are there because they love you – and as much as you don't want to hear all this soppy stuff in a book on a gangster tip, I'm afraid it's all true. But you can't do half of it 'cos you've got the other half as well. The other half of the rules where naughty men are concerned is that you treat your lady with more respect than you treat your fucking self – Rule Number One.

I have actually met a Swedish lady who was a paid assassin and had some heavy moments in Brazil. She'd been on some very major hits. Only about twenty-six. And one of the best bonks I ever had. She was another one who walked with an air of confidence and I'm sure with her training in the army special forces she was as deadly as you could get, more so for coming in such attractive wrapping. That's half the battle with women in a fight with a man 'cos the nicer they look the less you expect to get damaged by one.

Women play the mind game too, better than anyone else. And they can carve your knob off, stab you, set you on fire, kill your dog and then go, 'Sorry! PMT!' Best fucking alibi in the world. You could actually top someone once a month.

In case anyone's interested, the lady from the Dutch story in *Stop the Ride . . .* — the one that I took out of that mental situation I ended up in — she has been in touch. She managed to get through to my pal Marcus (who had helped us when we'd got back) and let him know that she was all right and that the secret was safe with her. The police still think they have enough of the story — film of us leaving the country and getting on the ferry, ID of the cars, and someone of the right description on the missing persons list — and they think my book fitted in the other bits at the end by telling them what happened over there. But because there is no body, and no weapon, and no witnesses they can't pull me in on it. That must be very frustrating for them!

I think it could have easily been a woman behind the murder of Jill Dando. I know what Jen would want to do if Jill Dando went on telly on *Crimewatch* and said, 'Have you seen this man? Call this number and get a reward,' you know what I mean? There's only so many women of men that have been nabbed and jailed that are gonna stand for that. Dando's expecting to put a thousand men in prison and not piss off all the wives and birds? These are the ladies of geezers who easily know how to get hold of people who do that kind of work.

They can't make it public knowledge that they might think it's the relative of someone banged away because of *Crimewatch* 'cos that undermines the whole grassing-people-up culture that they're trying to encourage. It would scare too many people off from ringing in.

You still can't put it past me that it wasn't a woman that was behind it all.

So the reason women can break you is because when it's all going right they can make you. The worst of a man can come out because of a woman, and also the best.

Then there's my Jennifer, who has all those different bits of toughness and then some, *and*, on top of all that, is very, very sexy with it. Also, living with me and not sticking a knife in me half the time has got to be worthy of every medal going.

Remember, the missus of this world often know where the bodies are and what was put in what hole. That's power in itself. Not forgetting, of course, the ultimate boss, which is your ma. Like I say, honour your father — fear your mum.

I get all the pats on the back and all the credit for being Dave Courtney but the truth is that my missus is 51 per cent of it. Jen is the spine, the core . . . she is everything. If that bit goes wrong at home then everything goes boss-eyed. My promise to Jen is this: I will make her laugh from the minute she wakes up in the morning to the minute she goes to bed, and I will make everyone else around me happy too, even if it's a real shitty position we're in. Just to keep the good humour going and keep the morale high is more important than ammunition.

And as long as everything's happy behind closed doors then I can fight the world.

18 MUM KNOWS YA

Your mum sees you as a little baby and then as a boy, when you're too naïve to hide your bad points. If you're cheeky, you're cheeky, and she sees it. If you're sneaky, you're sneaky; she sees it (even if you think she doesn't). If you're the jealous type, she sees that. If you're naturally lazy, she knows that. They know, mums. Because back then you hadn't yet *learned* to hide it.

As you grow older she also sees you grow more clever and more aware, and sees you trying to hide the bits you know people don't like about you, or the bits they don't like to see. Then you get to eighteen and you think you know it all. And you think your mum's forgot. Your mum ain't forgot, mate. She's just smiling to herself.

She knows your core 'cos she's seen it grow. Why do you think so many baddies are good to their mums!

So, if you've got more bad in you than good, and you get caught, and your mum gets called as a character witness . . . you'd better hope she's a *fucking* good liar.

19 RED SHOES, I'VE HAD A FEW

I'd like to say I regret nothing and that I'd do it all the same but, like the song said, 'Regrets, I've had a few, but then again too few to mention'; and that just about sums it up. But my biggest regret is this: I really wish that for those poxy few years that I was at school that I'd taken some interest, and for six hours a day let them teach me English, maths, language, etc., so that for the rest of my life I could benefit from it.

It wouldn't have changed me in what I wanted to do because I was gonna go *at it* from the minute I knew how to undo something. It wouldn't have changed my life but it would've made me an awful lot of a better one if I could read and write and speak another language. So, I regret not learning. That is my biggest regret, that I didn't do what I should've done at school. I'm now trying to teach my kids that.

Would I change my life now? No, I wouldn't. Not one bit.

Oh, wait a minute. Tell a lie, I've just remembered something. I bought a pair of red shoes last year for a hundred and twenty quid and I've never worn them. And I *knew* I'd never wear them! . . .

Apart from that, no regrets.

20 HONOURS AND GONERS

FIRST LADY
Jennifer

THE CLAN
Courtney, Beau, Levi, Chelsea, Genson, Drew, Patrick, Sue, Mum

THE BOLLOCKS
Bruce Reynolds, Joey Pyle, Fred Foreman, Charlie Richardson, Albert Chapman, Wilf Pine, Ronnie Biggs, Roy Shaw, Tony Lambrianou

FULLY FLEDGED MEMBERS
Seymour, Terry T, Dave L, W Bernie, Adam, Marcus, Cas, Ian F, Amon, Memmy, Big Steve, Steve R, Steve W, Pete, Ben, Ben W, Frankie, Ray, Andy, Andy B, Lenny, Kenny, Manny, Danny, Wolfie, Warren, Warwick, Wish, Ricky, Rocky, Ronnie, Johnny, Billy, Billy G, Clint, Creed, Glenn, Terry, Don, Dean, Daniella, Jackie, Lloyd, Floyd, Norris, Colin, Rod, Mickey, Al, Jack, Tony, Les, Joe, Big Reg, Christian, Mel, John, John E, Johnny G, Jo, George, Sid, Dave, Kerry, Jenny, Faz, Jamie, John, Rob, Brian, Jamie, Neil, Noel, Jonathan, Mark, Marc, Marky, Pat, Baz, Lee, Linda, Cary, Gary B, Denis, Chris, Chris L, Tommy, Ian, Mick, Paul, Carl, Tony T, Ian I, Jack, Chas, Errol, Selwyn, Oliver, Nigel, Norman, Nick, Warren, Laurence, Lou, Zak

MOST OUTSTANDING MEMBER
Mine

BEST SUPPORTING MEMBER
Viagra

THE 'YOU KNOW WHO YOU ARE' AWARDS ...
To the Liverpool lads, the Glasgow boys, the Newcastle and Sunderland fellas, the Yorkshire chaps, my Welsh crew, the Birmingham boys, the Irish supporters, the Portsmouth ones, the London posse, and the rest of you who 'know who you are'...

BEST SCARY EYES
Mad Pete

FUNNIEST GEEZER WITH HUGEST ARMS AWARD
Big Marcus

THE 'STILL LOOKS MEAN EVEN WHEN EATING A POT NOODLE OSCAR
Wish *(see Channel 5 documentary 'Dave Courtney's Underworld')*

BEST KARAOKE
Charlie Bronson's 'What A Wonderful World'

THE ROBIN De BANKS AWARD FOR MOST COLOURFUL NAME
Johnny Jacket, American Pit Bull Steve, Warrior, Lone Wolf, Wish, Wolfie, Cowboy, Caesar the Geezer, Fred the Head, Mad Dog Mangan, Mickey Gold Tooth, Action Man, Timmy Ram Jam, Dominic Spreadlove, Attitude, Outcast Phil, Terry Turbo, The Priest, Ricky Too Hard, Little Legs

HONORARY DIAMOND GEEZERS
Eammon O'Keefe, Vinoo, Dave Ford, Harry Hayward, Fidel Castro, Winston Churchill

FROM FIGHTERS TO WRITERS: THE PEN IS MIGHTIER
Norman Parker, Geoff Thompson

THE 'IF IT MOVES FUCK IT' COMMEMORATIVE CHASTITY BELT LOCK-PICKING KIT
Brendan

THE MAN MOST OUTSTANDING IN HIS FIELD
A farmer (who else do you know who has a field)

THE RODNEY KING AWARD FOR PERSISTENT POLICING
The Metropolitan Police

THE GARETH SOUTHGATE ACCURACY AWARD
The Metropolitan Police

BEST BULLSHIT DETECTORS
The jury

TO THOSE NOW GONE
Francis, Charlie, Reg, Ron, Lennie, Big Ron

Look out for other compelling True Crime titles from Virgin Books in 2002:

Killers on the Loose – Unsolved Cases of Serial Murder
by Antonio Mendoza
Revised and updated edition
January 2002
£6.99

According to a recent FBI study of serial murder, it has climbed to an 'almost epidemic proportion'. It is believed there are currently up to 6000 people a year dying at the hands of serial killers. The FBI and other law enforcement agencies estimate that there are between 35 and 50 serial killers on the loose at any given time. Other estimates put the number of killers closer to 500. In either case, officials expect these numbers to continue their dramatic rise. This is an up-to-date edition of an original in-depth study of serial killers at large, written by one of the world's foremost authorities.

ISBN: 0 7535 0681 5

Crossing To Kill – The True Story Of The Serial-Killer Playground
by Simon Whitechapel
Revised and updated edition
February 2002
£6.99

Since 1993 over 180 women have been raped and brutally murdered in Ciudad Juárez, a Mexican border town notorious for its pollution and overcrowding. Despite a number of arrests, the killing won't stop. Authorities suspect that killers are coming from all over Mexico - and even crossing the border from the USA - to rape and kill with impunity. Simon Whitechapel conducts a detailed analysis of the contributory factors surrounding these brutal slayings and looks at the turbulent cultural history of this often-violent country. Is there any way to protect women from this playground for serial killers?

ISBN: 0 7535 0686 6

Jack The Ripper, The Final Chapter
by Paul H Feldman
March 2002
£6.99

A haunting journal that came to light in 1991 and was published in 1993 as *The Diary of Jack the Ripper*, was believed to be a hoax. Yet no one was able to explain how it was forged, or by whom. The reason, as Paul Feldman explains, is because the journal is genuine. In this exhaustively researched and most extensive Ripper investigation ever undertaken, Paul Feldman cuts through the cover-ups and wild theories surrounding the Ripper mystery to undoubtedly prove that James Maybrick was Jack the Ripper. As well as uncovering crucial new evidence about the murders, Feldman presents sensational revelations from the Ripper's living descendants.

'... my own feeling was that Feldman has taken game, set and match.'–

Colin Wilson

ISBN: 0 7535 0637 8

**Raving Lunacy: Clubbed to Death – Adventures on the Rave Scene
by Dave Courtney**
Hardback published October 2000/Paperback published March 2002
£16.99/£6.99
Notorious in London's criminal underworld, Dave is also a big name
in the club and dance scene. *Raving Lunacy* is the story of this
double life, and how one world spilled over into the other. From
illegal parties in prisons, sewers, railway arches and aircraft
hangars to award-winning legitimacy, *Raving Lunacy* covers the
ground that *Stop the Ride* left out, as Dave details what went on
after the doors were shut tight. And of course the clientele that
came to the parties was, in Dave's words, 'the most colourful
characters London has to offer'. Dave was, as ever, in the thick of it
and saw and experienced the explosions, the fallout, the casualties
and the successes. Told with characteristic humour and brazen
honesty, *Raving Lunacy* reveals the darker side of the era known as
the summer of love.

ISBN: HB 1 85227 901 X/PB 0 7535 0504 5

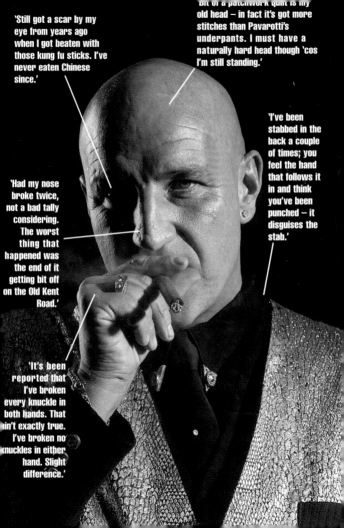

'Still got a scar by my eye from years ago when I got beaten with those kung fu sticks. I've never eaten Chinese since.'

bit of a patchwork quilt is my old head – in fact it's got more stitches than Pavarotti's underpants. I must have a naturally hard head though 'cos I'm still standing.'

'I've been stabbed in the back a couple of times; you feel the hand that follows it in and think you've been punched – it disguises the stab.'

'Had my nose broke twice, not a bad tally considering. The worst thing that happened was the end of it getting bit off on the Old Kent Road.'

'It's been reported that I've broken every knuckle in both hands. That ain't exactly true. I've broken no knuckles in either hand. Slight difference.'

'I didn't need that little wiggly bit on the side of my ear anyway. Good job 'cos someone bit it off.'

'This nutter went berserk and started ripping through my clo with his teeth and then biting chest like an animal!'

'This bloke pulled out a flick knife a threw it at me. I think he was as gobsmacked as when the blade actually stuck in my arm!'

'Got a knife stuck into my right arm by a gypsy. It got jammed in the elbow bone joint and just stuck there! Even I thought wow!'

'I was selling a bulletproof vest decided to test i My mate Ian seiz the chance to sh me and get away with it! So he fir into the vest and really hurt – I he a rib snap.'

'These little piggies of mine nearly didn't go to market when my fingers got cut with a cleaver – not a bundle of laughs!'

'Yeah, I got stabbed in my arse! I got a dead arse – I could have sat on a hedgehog with a hard-on and ne felt it.'

'I got shot in the knee, but fortunately it was a .22 so I just got a bit of metal stuck in me instead of losing half my leg.'

'This is where I got shot in the shin by a 9mm Luger.'